W hat about you? Do you ever think about getting married?

He glanced at her, but she was gazing out the window, as if only mildly interested in his answer. *All the time since you came home. If things were different....* "I'd like to get married someday and have a couple of kids, but I'm in no rush. How about you?"

She turned, meeting his gaze. For an instant, he saw stark loneliness in her eyes, then her expression changed as she tried to hide her feelings. He heard a trace of wistfulness in her voice when she answered. "I think about it sometimes. I'm not sure I could handle marriage and my career. Some folks do it, but a lot of them don't. The last thing I want is to make a promise I can't keep."

Palisades.
Pure Romance.

FICTION THAT FEATURES CREDIBLE CHARACTERS AND

ENTERTAINING PLOT LINES, WHILE CONTINUING TO UPHOLD

STRONG CHRISTIAN VALUES. FROM HIGH ADVENTURE

TO TENDER STORIES OF THE HEART, EACH PALISADES

ROMANCE IS AN UNDILUTED STORY OF LOVE,

FROM BEGINNING TO END!

A PALISADES CONTEMPORARY ROMANCE

LOVE SONG

SHARON GILLENWATER

PALISADES

This is a work of fiction. The characters, incidents, and dialogues are products of the author's imagination and are not to be construed as real. Any resemblance to actual events or persons, living or dead, is entirely coincidental.

LOVE SONG
published by Palisades
a part of the Questar publishing family

OCT 27 1995 © 1995 by Sharon Gillenwater
International Standard Book Number: 0-88070-747-X

Cover illustration by George Angelini
Cover designed by David Carlson and Mona Weir-Daly
Edited by Shari MacDonald

Printed in the United States of America

For information:
QUESTAR PUBLISHERS, INC.
POST OFFICE BOX 1720
SISTERS, OREGON 97759

95 96 97 98 99 00 01 02 — 10 9 8 7 6 5 4 3 2 1

To the Lord for opening new doors,
and to Ted
for thinking of me and making
that phone call.
And in loving memory of Dick Foslin—
we miss your wit, your laughter, and
your sweet, gentle spirit,
but we know Jesus delights in having you
with him.

But I trust in your unfailing love;
my heart rejoices in your salvation.
I will sing to the LORD,
for he has been good to me.
Psalm 13:5-6 (NIV)

One

❧

Soaking up the bright sunshine of a March afternoon, Andrea Carson glanced up and down the deserted Main Street of Buckley, Texas. Sitting on the curb, she watched a baby whirl-wind romp across the dirt lot of the farm implement company on the next block, playing peek-a-boo behind big, green John Deere tractors and tall cotton strippers.

She had been away ten years, but some things hadn't changed. As her grandfather was fond of saying, they rolled up the sidewalks at five o'clock in the evening and put them back down at nine the next morning, except on Sundays, when they didn't bother with them at all. Jackson's Hardware and Feed Store was on the west end of town. Three blocks to the east, Greene's Grocery—still the only store open seven days a week—marked the other end of the business district.

Findley's Apothecary sat midway between them, with its dark red brick walls and a faded green canvas awning shading the front. Andi couldn't remember when the awning had been bright green. No one else seemed to, either. The drug store was closed on Sunday, but if someone needed a prescription filled, Mr. Findley's phone number was posted on the door. If he wasn't home, the customer was instructed to call his daughter, and she'd find him—usually at the lake with a fishing pole in his hand. Andi smiled. Buckley's version of call forwarding had been around long before that type of service reached the big cities, and it didn't cost a penny extra.

But many things had not remained the same. The post office, library, and Citizens Bank—all a block north of Main Street— were the only other occupied buildings downtown. The rest of the store fronts were vacant. The Five 'n' Dime, where she had spent practically every cent of her baby-sitting money on country music cassettes, had closed the year she headed for Nashville. Knox's Department Store, where old Mr. Knox had tucked away the prettiest blue prom dress this side of heaven just for her, had closed a year later. Over time, the other businesses had simply faded away. Buckley looked as worn out as she felt.

A sudden gust of wind sent a chill clear through her. Andi turned up her collar and pulled her coat sleeves down over her hands. It was only four blocks back to her cousin Dawn's house, but she didn't think she had the strength to walk that far.

"Dumb, Andi. Real dumb. After more than a week in bed, you should have stayed in the yard," she muttered. Down the street, a beige pickup truck backed out from Greene's Grocery, but she barely noticed. Two-thirds of the pickups in West Texas were some shade of pale brown. She'd always figured it was so the dirt wouldn't show as much. Cupping her chin in one hand, she leaned her elbow against her knee and wondered if the sheriff would arrest her if she fell asleep on the sidewalk. "At least then I wouldn't be so bored," she said with a sigh.

Even as she spoke the words, she knew her problem wasn't boredom. It didn't matter if she were center stage in a sold-out concert hall or the only person on a Buckley street corner, she would be just as lonely, her heart just as empty. *It will be better when I'm well,* she thought, closing her eyes. *It has to be.*

Wade Jamison stepped on the brake, slowing his pickup, and stared at the woman sitting forlornly on the curb. He'd dreamed of her so many times, especially during the first few years after she left, he could recognize her even a block away. Her dark brown hair was shorter than it had been when they were in high school, but he had noticed that the first time he saw her in a music video. Instead of flowing across her shoulders, it fell from a center part to slightly past her chin, framing her face in a gentle sweep of soft, rich velvet.

He eased the truck to a halt in the middle of the street and quietly rolled down the driver's side window. She was too thin, yet more lovely than ever—sweet, beautiful Andrea, whose smile had once been the only brightness in a world of gloom. The most popular girl in school, she should have ignored the awkward, shy boy who moved to Buckley the second month of their senior year. But she hadn't. When he'd been assigned the seat beside hers in English class, her welcome had been warm and genuine. Over the next few weeks she had become his friend.

And Wade had fallen in love.

As he studied the delicate features that had haunted his memory for so many years, an intense longing swept over him. Heart pounding, he glanced away. Andrea had never known how he felt about her. He'd never even asked her out. The first time he heard her sing, he knew she was destined for a world far bigger than Buckley, Texas. *Easy, cowboy,* he chided himself. *You're not a kid anymore. Don't go wishin' you could rope the moon.*

Taking a deep breath, Wade looked back at her and frowned. She appeared exhausted and still hadn't opened her eyes. He shifted into park and turned off the engine. "Hey, songbird, you're gonna get arrested for vagrancy," he called softly.

Her eyelids fluttered open, and she blinked a couple of times, obviously disoriented. Then her gaze fell on him, and a smile lit her face, flooding his heart with sunshine. "Wade!"

She stood with effort and walked slowly toward the pickup. The sickly pallor of her fair skin worried him, as did the dark circles beneath her big, brown eyes.

"Did you take the wrong exit off the freeway?" he asked with a smile, resting his arm along the open window of the truck. "I thought you were supposed to be up in the Pacific Northwest about now."

A hint of unhappiness flickered across her face, then she smiled again, dimples appearing in each cheek. "You keeping tabs on me, Jamison?"

"Yes, ma'am. Got to keep up with Buckley's most famous person." Everyone in the county knew that her three albums had hit the top of the country music charts and that her last two had each sold over a million copies. Two years earlier, she had been nominated for the Country Music Association's prestigious Horizon Award, given to the industry's most promising new artist. Folks in Buckley had been glued to their television sets during the awards ceremony. When she didn't win, many of the women cried, and more than one man growled a threat to go to Nashville and "give 'em what-for."

Wade held out his hand, and Andi laid hers in his open palm, squeezing gently. He wrapped his fingers around her icy ones. "You're freezing!"

"The wind is colder than I thought it would be."

Wade released her hand. "Get in. It's warm in here." Andi stepped back as he got out of the truck. Moving past him, she grabbed hold of the steering wheel, put one foot inside on the floor, and hoisted herself up toward the high seat, barely reaching it. When she teetered on the edge of the seat, he quickly stepped up to steady her, resting his hand on her back, bracing her body against his, so she wouldn't fall. She was trembling. "You okay?"

"Pretty wobbly. I'm getting over a bout of pneumonia. Guess I shouldn't have ventured out so soon." She glanced up at him, her eyes revealing not only her weariness but also a deep sadness.

"Rest a minute. I'm not in any hurry."

She whispered her thanks and relaxed against him, laying her head on his shoulder.

"I've been down in Mexico and out of touch with most of the world for the past three weeks," he said. "Just got home last night, otherwise I probably would have heard that you've been sick. Are you staying with Dawn?"

"Yes. Got here on Thursday. Doctor said I needed rest and peace and quiet."

"I'm not sure how much of that you'll get at Dawn's. That gal's got more go than the Energizer Bunny."

A smile touched her face. "She can tone down when she wants to. Besides, she's out of town at a big antique show. She's had her booth reserved for ages."

Wade was quiet for a few minutes, giving her a chance to rest. "Did you have to cancel the rest of your tour?"

She nodded. "Fourteen shows. My manager is trying to reschedule as many of them as he can. Missing them took a big bite out of our paychecks. The boys in the band were real nice about it, but I feel rotten. Some of the guys have families, and I know they needed the money, but they wouldn't let me pay them until we do the shows. At least the rest of the crew took their full checks. I never realized how hard it could be, having so many people depending on you."

Her voice trailed off, and Wade fought the urge to put his arms around her and promise her that he would make everything all right. He had never known Andrea to be dejected. She had met every situation head-on, changing course if necessary, but always with unflagging enthusiasm and determination.

God had given him a deep compassion and sensitivity to the pain of others, but the ache in his heart went far beyond that gift. His turbulent emotions surprised him. He was ready to move mountains or play David to some unknown Goliath—anything to protect her, to shield her from harm. To his dismay, Wade realized he was still very vulnerable where this woman was concerned. Perhaps even more so than ever. *I know we didn't meet here by chance, Lord,* he prayed silently. *And I know she can never be mine, but let me be here for her. Show me how to help her.*

He inhaled deeply, trying to calm down—and only succeeded in breathing in the heady sweetness of her fragrance. "You still wear the same perfume," he said softly, and instantly wanted to kick himself. She straightened and looked up at him, her expression filled with wonder. As she scooted over to the passenger's side, he climbed into the cab and smiled, hoping to cover his blunder. "Is it still the only kind that doesn't make you sneeze?" She nodded, and he forged on as he shut the door. "Remember when ol' Pete made such a big deal out of giving you that quart bottle of cologne for your birthday and insisted that you put some on right then? What was it called?"

"Night Fantasies. It was horrible."

"It worked as a room deodorizer, even if it did smell kinda like moldy pine needles. At least it covered up the stink from the rolls the lunchroom lady crispy crittered."

"I didn't notice. I was sneezing too hard." Andi laughed and met his twinkling gaze. He'd always had beautiful hazel eyes, a combination of brown and green, but she didn't remember them ever being so warm, so tender. He had been good at hiding his emotions, only once mentioning his parents' divorce, bitterly admitting that he had moved to Buckley to live with his aunt and uncle on their ranch because neither of his parents wanted him around. The Wade Jamison she had known had been deeply hurt and so painfully shy that he barely spoke to anyone. He had looked so lost and miserable that first morning in class that she couldn't have ignored him any more than she could have turned away a starved puppy in the middle of a hailstorm.

"What were you doing in Mexico?"

"My dad was involved in some charity work at several village hospitals. I tagged along to keep him company and help out where I could." He smiled. "His specialty is surgery. Mine is slappin' on paint or fixing leaky roofs."

Andi suspected roofs weren't the only things he could fix. He had a way about him, a gentleness that she had barely glimpsed when they were younger. Looking back, she realized they hadn't spent a great deal of time together, although she had considered him a good friend. She'd had a lot of friends and had often been in the middle of a group, but Wade's shyness kept him on the outside.

He had definitely changed for the better. Apparently he had resolved his differences with his father since he spoke of him with affection. Not only was he relaxed and confident, with an easy smile, but his once-gangly frame had filled out nicely. In spite of her tiredness moments before, she had been very aware of the hard, muscular chest she was leaning against. With the additional weight, his face was no longer too thin nor was his nose too prominent. Wade Jamison had become a very handsome man.

Too handsome to be unattached. Andi was surprised at her disappointment. She glanced down at his hand. No wedding ring. Lots of married men didn't wear wedding bands, especially when they worked with their hands. Was it possible some woman hadn't nabbed him?

She tapped his hard stomach. "Looks like somebody's cookin' agrees with you."

He chuckled. "Just Aunt Della's."

"What? No ladies trying to reel you in?"

A faint blush touched his cheeks. "Oh, I manage to get invited to dinner now and then. And I return the favor, but there's nobody I'm especially attached to."

A bright red mini-van pulled up beside them and stopped. The left front window slid down smoothly, and an elderly lady peered out. Her pure white hair was drawn up in a tight bun on the top of her head, but her deep blue eyes were just as clear and sharp as Andi remembered from senior English class. "Giving driving lessons in the middle of Main Street, Wade?"

"No, ma'am, Miss Atkins. I'm picking up a hitchhiker." He leaned back so their former teacher could see Andi more clearly. "You never know who you'll find wandering around downtown."

"Good afternoon, Andrea. I'm sorry that you're ill. From your appearance, you should still be in bed. You're as peaked as bleached bones."

"My thoughts exactly," whispered Wade.

"Gee, thanks," Andi mumbled back. "You're probably right, Miss Atkins. I was going stir crazy, but I think I tried to walk a little too far."

"Of course, I'm right. I heard on the radio that you're suffering from anemia and exhaustion as well as trying to recover from pneumonia. They didn't know where you were, or if they did, they weren't saying. Now, let this handsome young man buy you dinner—he can probably afford a hamburger or two, but you'd be better off with liver. Then you take her right home, Wade Jamison."

"Yes, ma'am," they answered automatically and in unison, then both laughed. Miss Atkins merely nodded in approval.

"I like your van," said Andi, barely hiding her amusement. "But I never thought you'd get rid of your old '49 Hudson."

"I still use it to drive to church, but now that I'm retired, I wanted something a bit more modern to take on trips." She grinned, her eyes dancing with merriment. "This one has all the bells and whistles." With that comment, she pushed a button, automatically rolling up the window, and drove off to the tune of "The Eyes of Texas are Upon You" blaring from a special horn.

"I don't believe it! What happened to her? Except for her hair turning white, she looks just like she always did, but she sure doesn't act the way she used to." Andi shook her head. "I would never have imagined her driving a red mini-van."

"She bought it the day after she retired. Said she'd challenged all the minds she could and molded as many lives as she cared to, that she'd been a straight-laced, prune-faced spinster school teacher long enough, and it was time to have some fun." Wade rolled up the window and started the truck, driving down to the next cross street and turning around. He flipped on the heater as he continued, "She's done a lot of traveling in it. Went to Mexico last fall and is planning to drive across Canada this summer. She goes country line dancin', too. Picks places where they have good music but don't get too rowdy. She's still a proper lady."

Andi stared at him. "You can't be serious."

"I am." He nodded as if he were sharing some profound wisdom. "From what I hear, she does some real mean boot scootin'. Of course, her boyfriend probably has something to do with it." He turned at the grocery store and headed toward the north side of town.

She eyed him warily, uncertain as to whether or not he was pulling her leg. "Who's her boyfriend?"

"Old man Garner."

"The *undertaker?*"

"The one and only. He doesn't look much like an undertaker when he's all decked out in his Western duds. And they really aren't so old. Barely sixty, I think. They're nice people. I'm glad they've found each other. I think it would be sad to live to a ripe old age and never have someone special—someone to care for who cared about you."

Andi leaned her head against the back of the seat, wondering if in a way she were like Miss Atkins. For ten years, her career had been the only thing that mattered. All her energy, time, and thoughts had been focused on becoming a success. She had achieved her goal, at least a good measure of it, and found it hollow. Fame had not eased her loneliness; money had not filled the emptiness in her soul. She kept telling herself that things would be better when she got well. It had become a litany to keep her going, something to cling to when she wracked her mind for new music and found nothing. Would she wind up rich and famous, but all alone? Would she discover at the end of the road that it was all for nothing?

Dimly, she realized Wade had stopped the pickup. She pushed aside her dreary thoughts and looked around. They were parked in front of the Lazy Day, the hamburger joint where all the kids had gathered when she and Wade had been in high school. Judging from the crowd of young people present, things hadn't changed much. He shifted his position, leaning at a slight angle against the door, and casually laid his arm across the back of the seat. His eyes sparkled with amusement.

"So, what'll it be, songbird? Want a hamburger? Or shall we go all out and make it liver burger?"

Laughter bubbled up from deep within her soul. "Cheeseburger, a large order of fries, and a Cherry-Coke."

He took off his blue cap with "Jackson's Feed Store" printed on the front and tossed it on the dusty dash. Smoothing back his light brown hair, he said, "I don't know. Now, you're running into real money. Adding cherry flavoring to the Coke gets expensive."

"Only if they have to go to Washington and pick the cherries."

He chuckled and placed their order through the intercom next to the truck. Turning back to Andi, he smiled. "If you're good and eat all your dinner, I'll buy you a hot fudge brownie sundae for dessert."

Andi groaned. "If I ate that much, I'd never make it up the porch steps. You'd have to carry me."

"I think that could be arranged," he said softly.

Andi met his gaze and caught her breath. Mischief, warmth, and something intangible yet intriguing glowed in those hazel eyes. *I'll bet it could.* And if she read the signs right, he wouldn't mind it a bit.

Neither would she.

Two

"You did what?" Dawn Carson set an iridescent blue and purple Carnival Glass bowl on the kitchen table, admiring it for a second before pinning her cousin with her gaze. "How did you run into Wade Jamison when you were under doctor's orders not to set foot outside this house? Did he sneak in the back door and crash into you when you came down the hall?" The petite blond carefully inspected Andi and shook her head. "Nope, that can't be it. You'd be covered with bruises if you collided with that big galoot."

Andi laughed. "He's not a big galoot."

"Hmmm. Do I detect a bit of interest?" Dawn pulled another item from the box sitting on the ladder-back kitchen chair and carefully removed several layers of white tissue paper from around a matching Carnival Glass water pitcher.

"How many pieces of this did you find?" Andi leaned closer, admiring the slightly raised image of a peacock curving around the pitcher, the shimmering blue, purple, and green tail feathers spread in the shape of a regal fan.

"Just these two. Quit changing the subject."

"I'm not. I'll buy them from you."

"Nope."

"But they match the vase Grandma Henderson gave me."

"I know. That's why I'm giving them to you for your birthday. No, you don't have to wait ten months and don't get all weepy on me."

Andi's eyes grew misty anyway. They'd been doing that a lot lately. "Thanks, cuz." She ran her finger lightly over the bowl, remembering how much her grandmother had prized the vase her grandfather had won at the fair.

"I'm just glad I rescued them. I found them at a garage sale last week, and the little gal had no idea of their value. They were way under priced. She had inherited them from a great-aunt and thought they were pretty, but she needed money a lot more than fancy glassware. She was such a sweet little thing, very pregnant, and so excited about the baby." Dawn shook her head. "She was hardly more than a child herself. Couldn't have been a day over seventeen, and her husband might have been eighteen."

"Two bits you paid her what you could sell them for." Andi took a bite of apple and watched a faint blush spread across Dawn's face.

"Well, I didn't go quite *that* far, but I couldn't rob her."

Andi laughed. "Some antique dealer you are. I thought that was the whole idea—find a good deal, buy low, and sell high."

"It is, and that's what I try to do most every chance I get. But this time was different." Dawn sat down at the table and picked up a snickerdoodle cookie, nibbling on it.

"You just have a soft heart."

Dawn's expression grew thoughtful. "It was more than sympathy. God wanted me to help those kids, to share His love with them. He wanted them to know He had His hand on them, and that they, and their baby, were special to him."

Andi had the apple halfway to her mouth, but instead of taking another bite, she set it down on the table. "So now God talks to you? Out loud?" She cringed at the cynicism in her voice, but she couldn't buy what her cousin was saying.

Dawn smiled. "No. It's more like whispers in my heart."

"Word for word?"

"That time it basically was. Usually it's just a feeling, like letting my conscience be my guide or maybe intuition. Sometimes it's something more."

Andi snatched up the apple and chomped into it. She knew all about conscience. Hers had been working overtime for months. She shuddered inwardly to think what "something more" would be like—not that she was a particularly bad person, but she wasn't a saint, either.

She'd tried to keep going to church after she moved away from home, but eventually gave up. Working at a variety of jobs during the week and singing on Friday and Saturday nights had taken their toll. Sometimes she had worked on Sundays, too, and when she hadn't, it had been the only day to catch up on her sleep. She knew God couldn't have been pleased with some of the honky-tonks where she had worked during those desperate early years in the business. Later, when she began touring as the opening act for various big name performers and then became a headliner, she was almost always on the road.

God had seemed far away for a long time. She was sure that if he ever glanced her way, he had a frown on his face. Yet, she was curious to hear the rest of Dawn's story. "So how did you explain why you were giving her more money?"

"I said exactly what God told me to say." Dawn dunked another cookie in a small glass of milk and caught the bite in her mouth before it crumbled into the liquid.

"Just like that? No reservations or fear and trembling?"

"It wasn't easy, and I wasn't exactly eloquent, but I knew if I didn't do as God asked, I'd regret it, and we'd all miss out on a blessing. After I shared with her, she hugged me with tears running down her cheeks. Her husband blinked back some tears, too. She told me that every time they get low on money, God sends someone to help them."

Andi tossed the apple core toward a wastebasket sitting beside the back door, grimacing when it splattered on the floor a few feet short of the goal. Before she was half-way out of the chair, Dawn had retrieved it and dropped it into the wastebasket.

"That was the most pathetic throw I've ever seen, especially for somebody who used to be star of the girls' basketball team." Using a paper towel, Dawn quickly wiped up the apple juice and pulp left on the floor. Then she was at Andi's side, taking hold of her arm. "Come on, sickie, time for you to stretch out on the couch."

Andi obeyed gratefully. She laid down on the pale green sofa, resting her head on a plump pillow embroidered with multi-colored tulips, and let Dawn spread a bright yellow afghan over her.

"After your nap, you can tell me about meeting up with Wade."

"Sure." Andi smiled and drifted off to sleep, dreaming of tender, hazel eyes, and strong arms holding her tight. The dream changed, and she was dressed in a flowing, yellow silk gown. Her hair was covered by a matching gauze veil that sparkled with diamonds. Leaning out a window in an ancient castle tower, she threw red roses down to Wade who stood below. Dressed as a knight, with the sunlight glinting off the helmet he held in one gloved hand, he laughed as he caught each flower.

Behind him was a lush green meadow filled with people milling about. Suddenly legions of faceless, screaming fans stormed toward the castle. Still clutching the bouquet, Wade dropped his helmet and turned to defend her.

The crowd melted into a huge fire-breathing dragon. As Wade reached for the sword at his side, his armor disappeared. He stood weaponless against the onslaught, with nothing more than his cowboy shirt, jeans, boots, and a bouquet of wilted roses to protect him. The dragon issued a challenge, scorching the grass at her hero's feet. Wade took a step forward to meet his foe, and Buckley's antique fire engine roared across the meadow, siren blaring.

Andi sat up with a strangled cry. Disoriented, her heart pounding and skin damp, it took her a minute to realize the phone was ringing. Hearing the shower running and Dawn singing away, she untangled herself from the afghan and hurried to the telephone. Answering, she sank down in a nearby kitchen chair and tried to clear the fog from her brain.

"Hi, Andi. This is Wade." There was a tiny pause. "Did I wake you?"

"Yes." She shoved her hair back out of her eyes.

"I'm sorry."

He sounded so contrite that she smiled. "It's okay. I was having a nightmare anyway."

"Did you go out on stage and forget the lines to a new song?" he teased.

"Worse. Godzilla was after me. He was trying to flame broil everything in his path."

"That is bad. Did you get away?"

The warmth in his rich bass voice sent goose bumps skipping over her skin. There was no way she was going to tell him about his starring role in her dream. "I guess so. Old Number Two was rolling up to put out the fire when I woke up. I thought the ringing of the phone was the siren."

He laughed softly, and Andi closed her eyes, picturing his smiling face. She was surprised by how much she wanted to see him again. Since the phone was cordless, she walked to the living room and sat down in a yellow, rose print, overstuffed chair. Turning sideways, she laid her head against one fat chair arm and draped her legs over the other, feeling like a school girl with a new beau.

Wade asked about her day, if Dawn had gotten home, and if the antique show had gone well. They chatted several minutes longer about nothing important, and she wondered silently if he found the conversation as pleasant as she did.

"I have a meeting at church tomorrow evening at six," he said. "It shouldn't last too long, so I thought maybe I could pick up some barbecue and potato salad from the deli at Greene's and treat you gals to supper."

"That's nice of you, but you bought me supper last night."

"Well, I have to eat anyway, and I'd much rather share a meal with two pretty ladies than eat by myself." He was quiet for a long moment. "Unless you'd rather I didn't come by."

"I'd like to see you," Andi said softly. "I really enjoyed being with you yesterday."

28

"I enjoyed it, too." A trace of huskiness had crept into his voice. "So what do you want for dessert?"

"We'll provide salad and dessert."

"No, ma'am. You're not strong enough to cook, and Dawn is too busy."

"I'm strong enough to open some cans of fruit and slop whipped topping on it. And Dawn brought back some out-of-this-world brownies from Dallas. She's rationing them out very carefully, so there should be some left."

"Sounds delicious. Especially the fruit slop. If we don't eat all of it, the hogs will love it." He laughed. "I'll see you around seven."

Andi said goodbye, switched off the phone, and laid it on her stomach.

Dawn stepped up beside her, fluffing her short blond curls with a towel. Grinning, she picked up the phone and set it on the table next to the chair. "Don't even try to tell me you're not interested in Wade Jamison."

"I shouldn't be."

"Why not?" Dawn plopped down on the couch.

"Well, for one thing, I'm on the road about two hundred days a year."

Dawn shook her head and waved her hand, dismissing the problem. "You could work something out. He's as good as they come. Besides, the man is gorgeous."

Andi frowned, carefully studying her cousin's expression. "Am I stepping into the middle of something? Are you interested in him?"

"No, but like every other female in this town, married or

single, I happen to like looking at him. Wade and I are often involved on the same projects at church. We're good friends, but nothing more. He's a fine man, but he's not my Mr. Right. Actually, I've sworn off men. I think all the good ones are taken." She tossed her towel at Andi. "Now, 'fess up. How did you run into him yesterday, and what did you do? I want all the juicy details."

Andi laughed and told her about her excursion downtown and about having supper at the Lazy Day with Wade. She told how he had gone through the house when he brought her home, checking every nook and cranny to make sure she was alone, and waited on the front porch until he heard her lock the door before he left. When she had protested that no one locked their doors in Buckley, he had patiently pointed out something she knew very well but wanted to forget—she was no longer a typical citizen in a small, sleepy town; fame and fortune brought new concerns.

Some details she kept to herself—the comfort and security she had felt when she was with him, the pleasant warmth that rushed through her at the sound of his voice, and how eager she was to see him again. Those thoughts were too private, too unexpected and new to share with anyone—even Dawn.

Three

❧

Wade checked his watch for the third time in five minutes and turned in the direction of Dawn's street, meeting the chief of police coming from the opposite direction.

The peace officer stopped the car and rolled down his window. He glanced at Wade's dark blue Chevy Blazer and scratched behind his ear, his expression puzzled. "Wade, have you been driving around the elementary school for the last ten minutes or so? We got a call that some character in a dark van was casin' the joint."

Wade laughed ruefully. "I'm your character. I'm early for an appointment so I was killin' time." He'd been in such a hurry to finish the committee meeting at church that he'd volunteered to handle three jobs for the summer picnic. Afterward, he had rushed over to the grocery store and bought supper, then realized he was running a good fifteen minutes ahead of schedule. There was one thing he had learned about women—they were usually understanding if a man arrived a few minutes late, but they hated it if he showed up too soon.

The chief laughed. "More likely early for a date, and you don't want to seem too anxious."

After taking Andi home on Sunday, Wade had checked with the police chief to make certain he knew she was in town. The officer assured him that they had been notified before her arrival, and that they were patrolling the neighborhood. "Somethin' like that, only it's not really a date. I'm just visiting an old friend."

"Oh, yeah?" The chief didn't appear the least bit convinced. "Seeing Andi again?"

"Having dinner with her and Dawn."

"She feeling any better?"

"She said she was when I talked to her last night."

"Good. I haven't stopped by; didn't want to bother her. We've been keepin' a pretty close eye on the house. Her manager said she refused to let her bodyguard come with her."

Wade frowned. "Bodyguard?"

The police chief nodded. "Guess she can't go out in public without being mobbed, and he was concerned about her. I told him not to worry. The local folks will treat her kindly, and we don't get many people from out of town. We've been watchin' for strangers, especially ones with cameras. We're not about to let any of those tabloid people get close to her—or anybody else for that matter, unless she wants them to. Since you've got an *appointment,* I'd say she wants to see you." He winked. "Reckon it's up to you how close you get. Tell her I sure enjoy her singin'. Yes, sir. Mighty proud of that little gal."

Wade watched the other man drive away and took a deep breath to calm down. He knew Andi's fame made people want to see her and talk to her, but it hadn't occurred to him that she might need a bodyguard every time she went out. He drove down the street, pulling up in front of Dawn's house a few minutes later. Sitting in the darkness, he studied the house. Although the living room was well lighted, the heavy lace curtains and bright porch light made it impossible to distinguish who was inside. He gathered up the bag of food and a bouquet of carnations and climbed out of the Blazer, noting how well the street light illuminated the front and side yards. His concern for her safety eased somewhat.

He glanced at the teddy bear lying on the passenger seat. Although he had bought it for Andi, he had decided she might think he was silly to get her something so childish. He had gone back into Greene's and bought the flowers instead. He left the bear in the Blazer and strolled sedately up the walk, resisting the urge to bolt up the porch steps by reminding himself this was only a friendly visit.

When Andi answered the door and smiled up at him, he almost lost his voice. Those cute dimples and the warm, happy sparkle in her dark brown eyes sent his intentions of only being a friend into the stratosphere. He let his gaze skim over her, noting how the soft pink cotton sweater and matching slacks complimented her slim figure and brought delicate color to her face. Her hair was parted on the side and swept across her forehead in a gentle wave that ended in a soft swirl above her ear. The tips of the dark, silky strands brushed her jaw line, exposing her slender neck. Suddenly, he longed to bury his hands in her hair and kiss her.

Clamping down on his wayward thoughts, he returned her smile. "You're lookin' mighty fine tonight, ma'am," he said in an exaggerated Texas drawl.

"Why, thank you, kind sir." Andi stepped back, opening the door wider, and said in her best sugary, Southern-bell voice,

"Please do come in. We've been anxiously awaiting your arrival."

Wade laughed. "Starving, huh?"

"Yep." She laughed and shut the door. As he handed her a bouquet of variegated pink and rose carnations, she noted a hint of shyness in his smile and a touch of color on his face.

"I thought these might cheer you up," he said. "Since nobody knows where you are, I didn't figure you were getting too many get-well wishes. I debated between these and a box of chicken livers, but decided the flowers smelled better."

"Much better. And they're a lot prettier." Andi grinned, meeting his laughing gaze.

He followed her into the kitchen, greeted Dawn, and set the grocery sack down on the counter.

Once again Andi was struck by his rugged good looks and confidence as he leaned casually against the kitchen cabinet. He wore cowboy garb—blue striped Western shirt, faded blue Wrangler jeans, a hand-tooled leather belt with a silver buckle, and black boots—but she suspected he would be as self-assured dressed in an expensive suit.

She wondered if she was putting more into his kindness than he intended. Was she so lonely that she only imagined his interest? She stepped beside him and reached up in the cabinet for a vase. When her shoulder brushed against his arm, she felt a jolt clear through her—and it had nothing to do with static electricity. The laughter faded from his eyes, and she knew he felt it, too. "Thanks for being so thoughtful."

"Anytime. I just hope they don't make you sneeze."

"I don't have a problem with carnations."

He gazed at her so intently that Andi's legs grew weak. "Are you a makeup artist, or are you really feeling better?"

"Both. I still get tired too quickly and sleep a lot, but I haven't had a dizzy spell or headache since Sunday. I feel a little bit stronger every day." She eased away, moving to the sink and filling the vase with water. "Of course, I'm taking a ton of vitamins and iron supplements, so I should have the fastest recovery on record." She unwrapped the carnations and put them into the vase, inhaling their spicy-sweet fragrance with a smile. Looking up, she met his tender gaze. "Thank you."

"You're welcome." He straightened and quickly began removing waxed cardboard containers from the grocery bag. "Dawn, do you want me to put this in something?"

"That shallow casserole dish on the counter is for the barbecue. There's a bowl up in the cabinet to your right for the potato salad." Dawn came out of the walk-in pantry with a handful of paper napkins. "Do you want iced tea?"

"Sure, that would be fine."

After placing the flowers in the living room, Andi took the fruit salad from the refrigerator and put it on the table as Wade carefully poured the long, thin slices of barbecue brisket and sauce into the casserole dish. He dumped the potato salad in a bowl while Andi set the rolls he had brought on a plate. Dawn poured them each a glass of tea. When they sat down at the table, Dawn asked Wade to say the blessing. Andi had expected it, since her cousin said grace before each meal, but she hadn't expected Wade to take her hand in his.

"An old family tradition," he said, reaching across the table to hold hands with Dawn, too. "Aunt Della says it's a way of showing everyone at the table that they are welcome, both in the circle of fellowship and in lifting their hearts to God." He smiled as

Andi reached for Dawn's free hand. "When I visited them as a kid, I thought they only did it to keep me from fidgeting."

Andi almost laughed out loud. She'd never felt more like fidgeting in her life. She bowed her head and closed her eyes, trying to have a prayerful attitude, but it was difficult when she was so aware of Wade's firm hand enclosing hers. Seconds later, she felt as if she were hovering at the threshold of heaven, carried there by the love and respect resonating in Wade's deep voice as he talked to God.

"Heavenly Father, thank you for this food, and thank you for bringing Andi home to us for a while. Please be with her, Lord, help her to recover and meet her every need. In Jesus' name, amen." He released Andi's hand slowly, as if he didn't want to let go.

She wanted to cling to him forever.

"So how are the plans coming along for the church picnic?" Dawn took several pieces of brisket and a spoonful of sauce, then passed the dish to Wade.

He shook his head. "I'm in charge of cooking the burgers and clean up, which is no big deal, but somehow I wound up saying I'd buy all the food, too." He filled half his plate with barbecue and handed the still heaping casserole dish to Andi. He looked at Dawn, his expression hopeful. "Could I talk you into helping me? I don't know the first thing about buying for a crowd."

"Sure, I'll help. I've done it plenty of times. It's not so hard when hamburgers are the main course. Gets a little more complicated when we're putting on something fancy."

They finished filling their plates and began to eat. Before long, the discussion turned to Dawn's idea of establishing a city museum.

"I thought we already had a museum. Isn't it in that old building next to the bank?" With a slight movement of her wrist, Andi waved her fork in the general direction of downtown. She laughed when Wade playfully ducked.

"There's a pile of stuff there, but it quit functioning as a museum about four years ago. We have plenty of old things to put on display, but we need a bigger and better place to do it."

Wade ate the last of the fruit salad and looked at Andi. "This is too good to throw out to the hogs." He met her smile with one of his own, then turned his attention back to Dawn. "You got a place in mind?"

"Knox's Department Store would be perfect. It's big, in pretty good shape, and has a long history in itself. I'm not sure, but I think it may have been one of the first buildings in town. Mr. Knox took good care of it."

"You think his heirs might donate it to the city?"

"Maybe. I'm going to try and round up some other interested people and see if we can get something started. We'll probably need some kind of committee or museum board set up before we approach the city council and county commissioners."

"It'll be a lot of work."

Dawn grinned. "So isn't everything? Want to be my first board volunteer?"

Wade held up his hands and shook his head. "No thanks. I'm on more than enough committees right now. But when you get down to hammering and painting, let me know. I'll be glad to lend a hand."

"A museum next door to your antique store is a good idea," said Andi.

"Store? Are you opening up a place here in Buckley?" asked Wade.

"I hope to. I've purchased that little building next to Knox's. One reason I bought it is because I've been dreaming of having the museum on Main Street for a long time. Besides, it was cheap and has a beautiful plaster ceiling."

A short while later, they were nibbling on brownies in the living room when Wade's aunt called. He talked to her briefly and hung up the phone, his brow wrinkled in a frown. "I have to go. One of our mares is ready to foal, and she's having problems. The vet is on his way out, but I need to be there, too."

"Won't you take some barbecue? There's plenty left," said Dawn.

"No, you keep it. That way you won't have to cook for a few days. I wouldn't mind another brownie though."

Andi handed him one and walked out to the Blazer with him. Her gaze skimmed over the vehicle. "Nice. Is it new?"

"About a year old." Wade wished he had a dimmer switch for the street light. "I drive it when I want to impress the ladies."

"Are you trying to impress me, Wade?"

He stepped closer and shrugged. "Maybe a little. I'm doing pretty well financially, but it probably doesn't hold a candle to what you make in a year."

"Does that bother you?"

"No, and I hope it doesn't bother you. It doesn't matter to me whether you're rich or poor, I'd still care for you. You're my friend, Andrea. You were there when I needed you ten years ago, and I'm here for you now."

A strand of hair blew across her face. He brushed it aside,

tucking it behind her ear, and let his fingertips trail along her cheek as he withdrew his hand. "I'll always be here for you."

Her eyes widened slightly. Even in the shadows, he could see the longing there, a yearning for love fervently echoed in his heart.

He stepped back and opened the door to the Blazer. Climbing in, he rolled down the window. "Sorry I have to leave so soon."

She leaned against the door, her expression wistful. "I'm sorry, too."

Impulsively, he picked up the teddy bear and held it in front of him. "Cute, huh?"

Her face lit up. "He's adorable." Pursing her lips, she playfully pinched his cheek. "Does duh big cowboy like to snuggle wiff his teddy?"

He raised an eyebrow. "Not in the last twenty years or so." *Testing it at the store doesn't count.* He handed the stuffed animal to her, and she immediately hugged it. He grinned.

She held it up to the light. "He has the cutest face, and he's so soft and cuddly."

"Guess that's why I thought of you when I saw it." He almost groaned out loud. How had he let that slip out?

"Anybody ever tell you that you're sweet, cowboy?" she asked quietly.

"Yeah, at least a dozen times a day." He started the Blazer. "Go on in the house, songbird, so I'll know you're safe."

She attempted a smile, but as she turned away, clutching the teddy bear as if she were a lost little girl, he caught the shimmer of tears in her eyes. He ached to gather her in his arms and hold her tight. He knew she must miss her friends and busy lifestyle. *Right now she is sick, lonely, and separated from everything important to her. She'd probably be attracted to any man who showed her tenderness. Easy pickin's.*

When she was inside the house, he gunned the engine and sped down the street, barely slowing at the stop sign three blocks away. He was halfway to the ranch before he realized he was going twenty miles an hour over the speed limit. He shook his head and lifted his foot off the gas pedal. "Lord, I'm gettin' in deep here. I feel like a teenager in love, and now I'm driving like one. I'm blowing it, Lord. I don't know how to handle this situation. How can I ease her loneliness without hurting her? Or myself?"

Wade drove the rest of the way in silence, waiting for God's direction. A single thought kept running through his mind, but he didn't know if God was speaking to him, or if he only heard the anguished cry of his own heart.

Just love her.

CHAPTER

Four

❧

By Saturday, Andi could tell a definite improvement in her strength. Although she still grew tired quicker than normal, she wasn't worn out all the time. Yet, she couldn't seem to shake the blues. When she had seen the doctor in Sidell the day before, he told her not to worry—feeling down was common with anemia. He assured her that once she completely regained her health, she'd be the lively, enthusiastic performer she'd always been.

She wasn't so sure. Sitting alone in Dawn's living room, she gazed at her great-grandmother's 1906 Lester upright grand piano. Andi was well acquainted with its deep, rich tone. At one time, she would have gone to it the minute she got up, perhaps playing for an hour before hunger forced her into the kitchen. She looked over at her acoustic guitar in the corner, untouched since she had arrived. No song ran through her mind or sprang from her heart. Her once fervent desire to sing had disappeared. Music no longer filled her soul.

"Snap out of it, Carson." She jumped to her feet. "It's a beautiful day. Perk up." Dawn was at an estate sale in the next county and had invited Andi to go along. Although it sounded like fun, Andi was afraid she would get too tired and had declined. She didn't want her cousin to feel obligated to leave the sale until she was ready.

She walked out onto the back porch and stretched in the warm morning sunshine, continuing her self-directed pep talk. "You just need some fresh air and to do something besides sitting around, turning into a sofa squash."

Spotting a flower bed in need of weeding, she strolled down the steps and plopped on the grass beside it. The weeds were small and the ground soft from the rain two nights before. As she plucked the little villains from around the partially blooming red geraniums, some of her tension and frustration eased. A red cardinal landed in the elm tree nearby. Andi leaned back on her elbows and watched the bird watch her. "Good morning, pretty thing," she said softly. "Isn't spring nice?"

The bird flew away, but seconds later a gray and white mockingbird landed almost in the same place. He ran through a series of melodies, mimicking the calls and songs of other birds, repeating each one half a dozen times before going onto the next. Andi listened, smiling in pleasure.

For about the twentieth time that morning, her thoughts drifted to Wade. She hadn't heard from him since he left on Tuesday night. She went back to weeding the small flower bed, knowing he would come if she called him, wishing he would drop by on his own. Looking up at the now silent mockingbird, she asked, "Reckon he's waiting for me to call?" The bird tipped his head as if considering her question. "Maybe he thinks I don't want to see him." The bird serenaded her again.

She considered the possibility for a few minutes, then went

inside, washed the dirt and green weed stains off her hands, and looked up his number in Buckley's tiny phone book. Dialing the cordless phone, she glanced at the clock and wondered if he'd be home at eleven o'clock on a Saturday morning. He was, but he sounded sleepy when he answered on the fourth ring.

"Hi, Wade. This is Andi. I'm sorry if I woke you."

"I was awake. Just being lazy. Waitin' on the coffee."

His voice was deeper than usual, his speech slow and relaxed. Hearing the television in the background, she pictured him sitting on a couch, wearing old, faded jeans and a white T-shirt, with his hair still rumpled from sleep and his bare feet propped up on a coffee table. It was an image bound to make any woman's heart beat faster.

She heard a faint, but distinct, "beep, beep," in the background and grinned. "Are you watching cartoons?"

He chuckled. "Caught me. I still get a kick out of the Road-runner and that dumb Wile E. Coyote. How are you feeling?"

"Better, although I still run out of steam too fast."

"I was sitting here thinking about you."

The last traces of her gloomy mood evaporated as she walked into her bedroom and flopped down on the bed. "I'm not sure that's good, considering what you're watching." He laughed, and Andi felt a rush of pure happiness.

"I wasn't making any comparisons. I've been meaning to call you all week but haven't had the chance. Been getting home too late. We've had baby critters hatchin' out all over the place."

"How are the mare and foal?"

"Fine. Thanks to a good vet and plenty of prayer, they both made it. It was scary for a while, though. That little guy wanted to stay right where he was. We thought we might lose them both. A little filly arrived about three this morning. That's why I'm moving so slow. You doin' anything today?"

"Nope. Dawn is at an estate sale, and I'm down to talking to the birds."

"Are they talking back?"

"Well, Mr. Mockingbird had a comment, but I'm a little fuzzy on the translation."

"He was telling you to come out to the ranch and spend the day with me."

"Special air mail message, huh? I'd love to, but I'll need a ride. The doctor doesn't want me to drive for another week. I considered ignoring him and picking up a rental car anyway, but decided I'd better follow orders."

"I'll come get you, but don't dress up. I'd like to take you around the ranch, but we'll need to go in the pickup. It's a bit dusty inside."

Andi laughed. "I'd like to see a work pickup in this part of Texas that isn't. I don't mind a little dirt."

He made a funny noise, a cross between a yawn and a groan. Andi smiled, picturing him stretching the kinks out of his back. "Sounds like you need some more sleep."

"It just takes me a while to get my motor revved up."

She wondered why she found that so endearing.

"I can be there about a quarter after twelve, if that's all right."

"I'll be ready." She switched off the phone and dropped it on the bed, humming a happy little tune. She picked up the teddy bear from beside her and set him on her stomach, leaning him back against her bent legs. "Well, Sweet Thing, looks like I was

44

right to name you after that handsome cowboy."

She rested a while, ate a quick lunch, then primped a bit. She changed into a short sleeved, blue print cotton dress made in a basic a-line style that was loose and comfortable. She slipped on a pair of canvas flats before doing her makeup—a touch of mascara, blush, and lipstick. While brushing her hair, she heard the rumble of a car with a loud muffler coming down the street. When it stopped in front of the house, she hurried to the living room window. Wade was climbing out of a pristine, bright red roadster. She couldn't tell a Ford from a Chevy, but it was obvious that the old car had been lovingly restored.

Grabbing her purse and a light sweater, she raced out the door, barely remembering to close it. "Wade, it's beautiful! Is it yours?" His twinkling eyes and smug smile gave her his answer before he nodded. Andi walked around the car, admiring the spotless paint, sparkling chrome, and big round headlights perched atop the sweeping front fenders. Inside, the wooden steering wheel and dash were smooth and shiny; the red leather upholstery, soft and inviting. "What kind is it?"

"A '33 Chevy Coupe."

"Did you restore it yourself?"

"Yep. Spent about a zillion hours on it."

"And a ton of money."

He laughed. "Nearly. Haven't you heard? Men don't grow up; they just get bigger toys." He opened the passenger door and bowed slightly as she sat down. "It's not stock. I changed a few things, like adding a bigger engine and some other stuff to make it run better. And of course, I had to have a stereo, air conditioner, and seat belts."

After he closed the door, she watched him walk around the

front of the car and admired the way he looked in his buckskin colored Western shirt and jeans. Like most cowboys, he had a long, easy stride, with a hint of a swagger. The boots contributed to that walk, but they couldn't account for all of it. He was a man comfortable with himself; one who knew who he was and accepted it.

He met her gaze as he sat down. "What?" he asked softly.

"I was thinking how much you've changed since high school," she said, buckling her seat belt as he fastened his.

"I was pretty miserable back then. It took several years for Uncle Ray and Aunt Della to love away the hurt." He pulled onto the street and headed out of town. "Even then, they didn't do it alone. Finding Jesus was a big part of it, and finally sitting down and talking to my dad, man-to-man, helped, too." As soon as they were on the open road, he stomped on the gas pedal. With a roar of the engine and a surge of power, they reached the speed limit in seconds.

Andi laughed in delight. "How fast will it go?"

"As fast as a modern Chevy. I haven't tested it out. I have too much time and money invested in this little beauty to risk crashing her." He smiled mischievously. "Besides, I'm a wimp when it comes to pain, and Aunt Della doesn't put up with much moanin' and groanin'. I found that out when I was bull-riding."

"Sounds to me like you had a death wish." She meant to tease him but instantly regretted her words when his expression darkened.

"I did," he said quietly.

She laid her hand on his shoulder. "I'm sorry. I was only kidding, but I shouldn't have said that."

He felt her tender touch all the way to his toes. "It's all right.

46

You didn't know. It was the summer after we graduated. I was so bitter and angry with my parents that it seemed like a good way to work some of the venom out of my system. And, to be honest, I didn't care if I got killed in the process. It didn't seem like I had much to live for." *You were gone.*

"What happened?"

"I made it through several rodeos with only bruises, scrapes, and sore muscles. I even placed third a couple of times and thought I was hot stuff." He shook his head and smiled wryly. "But in San Angelo, I knew I was in big trouble even before we left the chute. That ol' bull rolled his head around and stared at me with eyes of fire. I was on his hate list, and he did his best to squish me right there in the chute. When they threw open the gate, he flew out like a tornado. He twisted and bucked and spun one way, then the other. We parted company about four seconds into the ride. I woke up on the way to the hospital with a concussion, two broken ribs, and a broken arm. It didn't take me long to figure out that gettin' killed wasn't worth the pain.

"Trouble was, I didn't know what to do to earn a living. Dad offered to pay my way through college, but I wasn't interested. I didn't want his money, and I had barely made it out of high school."

"Because your family life was such a mess. You're no dummy, Wade Jamison."

"Why, thank you, ma'am." He smiled, pleased with her compliment, and even more pleased that her hand still rested on his shoulder. "I liked working on the ranch better than anything else, but I knew I'd never make enough money as a cowboy to buy much of a place of my own. Uncle Ray and Aunt Della were real good to me, but I still felt like an outsider. I wanted it that way. I was afraid to love them. I didn't want to get hurt when they got tired of having me around."

"Which is what happened with your parents."

"That's the way I saw it then. Now, I realize how badly hurt Dad was when my mother walked out. He was having too hard a time handling his own pain to try to help me with mine, so he sent me to live here. It was a bitter, nasty divorce. He was actually trying to protect me, but I thought he didn't love me anymore." Her fingers tightened against his shoulder. He glanced at her, noting the tiny frown between her brows. "Don't frown. I don't want you getting wrinkles on account of me. Dad and I have a great relationship now."

"What about you and your mom?"

"Not so great."

He shrugged as if it didn't matter, but Andi sensed that the situation was still painful for him. She wanted to know more but didn't want to spoil their time together. Giving his shoulder a tiny squeeze, she moved her hand and shifted slightly, turning to look out the window. "Spring is my favorite time of the year in West Texas—if we've had a rain. Everything is so pretty and green. Am I seeing things, or are those wild flowers on the hill up ahead?"

As they sped down the highway, the flowers became more clearly defined. "You mean that great, big patch of yellow stuff?" asked Wade, leaning forward and squinting toward the small hill. "I think somebody's been out here with a can of spray paint."

"Maybe Mother Nature."

"More like Father God," he said quietly.

Andi gazed across the wide, open prairie, sighing in contentment. "He does know how to do panoramic landscapes, doesn't he?"

"That he does." Wade slowed the roadster and turned off the highway onto a paved road, driving beneath a wide, black wrought iron arch with the name "Smoking Pipe Ranch" worked into the pattern. A heavy wooden sign on the right side of the gate stated, "Ray and Della Jamison, Wade Jamison, Owners." The brand of a pipe with a snake-like trail of smoke rising from it was burned into the wood.

"Doesn't look like you're an outsider anymore."

"Nope. Half owner. Partly given, partly earned. When Uncle Ray saw I wasn't going back to the rodeo and intended to stay on at the ranch, he offered to teach me the business and pay me regular cowboy wages. He said if I stayed five years and proved my worth, he'd give me a quarter interest in the ranch. I kept my part of the bargain, and he kept his. I also took some college classes in business and range management and learned how to work a computer. It's a real benefit these days, but Uncle Ray won't touch it, so keeping the records has become part of my job. The part I don't particularly like. Thankfully, we have an accountant to do most of the number crunching.

"We've had some good years, and some of my investments paid off extremely well. Six months ago, I bought another quarter interest. That's plenty for me. When Ray and Della are gone, their grandson will inherit their share. He's only seventeen and lives in Houston with his folks. Ray's daughter and her husband own a thriving import business and aren't the least bit interested in the ranch, but that boy would be up here every weekend if he could get away. He's got ranchin' in his blood."

They went over a small rise in the road, and he stopped the car. Andi's gaze swept over the wide, shallow valley backed by low lying hills. The vivid, contrasting colors defining the shapes and patterns of the fields, pastures, and roads reminded her of a beautiful pieced quilt, one accented with embroidered trees, cattle, and buildings.

To the right, a rich green pasture spread across the gently rolling land, adorned with brilliant splashes of yellow and purple wildflowers beneath the bare brown trunks and branches of mesquite trees. Cattle of varying shades of red, brown, and black grazed in the pasture. She recognized the red Herefords with their white faces and a few Black Angus, but she had no idea what the brown ones were called.

A dirt road ran along the edge of the pasture, stretching nearly the length of the valley before it made a sharp turn to the left. Like perfectly spaced stitches, the posts and barbed wire of the fence seemed to hold the edge of the long brown ribbon in place, separating the multi-hued pasture from the almost solid green of one field and the reddish-brown of another. A second fence divided the curving lines of the freshly plowed field from the soft, green vegetation next to it.

Down a winding road to their left were the ranch house, barn, various sheds, corrals, and two smaller houses. With its freshly painted white siding and green roof and trim, the long, rambling single story ranch house seemed comfortable and welcoming. The wide expanse of native grass and sprinkling of wild flowers between the house and the weathered brownish-gray corral fences and out buildings added to the rustic charm. The smaller houses on the other side of the corrals were white with shiny tin roofs.

"Wade, it's beautiful." Andi smiled at his satisfied expression. "I can see why you love it so much. If I had a place like this, I think I'd stay here forever."

For a heartbeat, the burning intensity of his gaze took her

breath away. Then he looked back across the valley. "Where are you living now?"

"I have an apartment in Nashville, but I'm hardly ever there. Most of the time I'm either on the tour bus, or a plane, or in a hotel," she said with a sigh. "We toured over two hundred days both last year and the year before. Kyle wanted us to do even more this year, but I refused. This trip was supposed to be over at the end of March. We weren't going out again until August. Now, we'll have to try to make up some of the shows we missed as soon as I'm well enough."

"Who is Kyle?"

"My business manager. He's done a good job for me, making the right contacts and the right bookings, and he negotiated a fantastic recording contract. I wasn't going anywhere until I signed with him, just withering away in hundreds of nameless bars and honky-tonks across the country." A little shiver ran up her back. "My old manager kept telling me that I had to make a name for myself with the common folk. Believe me, the people in a lot of those places weren't like any of the common folk I grew up with."

Scowling, Wade glanced at her. "How bad was it?"

"Well, the worst places had heavy mesh wire around the stage to protect the band when the beer bottles and bodies started flying. It also separated us from our adoring fans." She smiled. "Of course, that didn't always stop my more adamant admirers. One time a tattoo-covered biker just whipped out a huge pair of wire cutters and started snipping away so he could pay me a visit. The guys in the band formed a line of defense, but all of them together wouldn't have been much of a match for him. Thankfully, the club had two Herculean bouncers who convinced him that it wasn't a good idea. The band members were as fed up as I was, and a couple of them weren't getting along, so we fired the agent and headed back to Nashville.

"I got a job as a tour guide at the Country Music Hall of Fame. The band broke up, and they all drifted to other groups. A few months later Kyle heard me sing at a benefit concert. He signed me up two days later, with the promise that I wouldn't have to play in any sleazy places. His organization put together a first-class band to work with me. The first year we still did occasional club gigs, but only the larger and nicer ones. Now, we don't do any at all."

"He works you too hard."

"He wants me to succeed."

"I thought you had."

"To a nice level, yes, but there is still room to grow. Maintaining what we've accomplished could be hard. Country music is hot right now—and while that means more opportunities, it also means there are more people trying to grab a piece of the dream. Seems like new, young stars spring up every month, many of them hitting the top of the charts with their first album."

"Just like you did."

"But I had been working toward it for a long time. Of course, a lot of other singers have, too, but there are quite a few who get their break within a year of moving to Nashville." She stared out the window, thinking of the endless stretch of highway waiting for her, the towns and faces and days and nights that all too soon became a blur. The loneliness.

"Andi?" Wade's soft voice held a note of concern.

"I'm not sure I can do it anymore. I don't even know if I want to."

"You're just not feeling up to snuff. Once you get your energy back, you'll do fine. You love it, and you know it. You run out on stage and greet the audience, and your face lights up like a neon sign. When you start singing and the place goes wild, you're right where you're supposed to be, bringing joy and pleasure to thousands of people. You give them a special gift with every song you sing."

"How do you know?" Andi pinned him with her gaze. He squirmed and put the car into gear.

"I'm a fan, silly. All your songs are special."

"Not that. How do you know what I look like when I step on stage?"

"I have a cousin in Boulder. I happened to be visiting him when you were there, and we went to the concert. Got good seats, too."

"That performance was sold out weeks in advance. How did you get tickets?"

"Bought them from a scalper standing out front. It was worth his price. You put on quite a show."

"Why didn't you come out to the bus for the Shake 'n' Howdy."

"What's that?"

"It's a time after the show when we talk to folks who have wrangled a backstage pass from our road manager. Usually they are people from the local radio stations and their contest winners, maybe family members and friends or sick kids who need a wish to come true, and always the die-hard fans. I try to visit with each of them for a few minutes." She paused. "Didn't you want to say hello?"

"Sure I did, but my cousin had to get up early the next morning for work."

"I wish you would have stopped by."

"I should have. I've regretted not doing it ever since. Speaking of stopping by, I hope you don't mind visiting with Aunt Della and Uncle Ray for a few minutes. They'll have my hide if we don't."

Five

D id he tell you we made him move out because of you?" The sparkle in Ray Jamison's eyes warned Andi that Wade's uncle was about to tell her another "this nephew of mine" story—the third or fourth in less than an hour.

She glanced at Wade, smiling in amusement and sympathy as his face turned pink. "No, I don't believe he mentioned it."

"Well, now, little lady, you need to understand that I don't have a thing against country music. In fact, I enjoy it. I have to admit that generally my tastes run more to the older singers, the ones I grew up with, but I'm not such an old fuddy-duddy that I can't enjoy some of this new stuff, too. And I particularly like your music."

"Thank you." Andi couldn't imagine anyone considering the older Jamison a fuddy-duddy. He was tall and slim with just a dusting of gray in his light brown hair. Time and the sun had etched a few creases in his face, but no doubt he still turned a few ladies' heads when he walked into a room. He looked enough like Wade to be his father instead of his uncle, and that he loved him like a son was obvious.

"I think he was at the head of the line to buy your first single record." Ray grinned and winked at Wade.

"It wasn't a very long line," she said with a laugh.

"I was as happy as a frog after a good rain when your second single came out, 'cause we had something else to listen to—over and over and over. Then he got your first album, and this nephew of mine decided he liked his music loud—real loud. He flat wore out a set of speakers and had to go get some more. When he came in from town, we met him at the door with the rest of his stereo and told him it was time to move on down the road."

"Don't let him kid you, Andi. I'd finished building my house and was moving out anyway." Wade grinned good-naturedly. "The stereo just happened to be the first piece of furniture to go."

Wade's aunt patted him on the arm. Della Jamison was a short, pleasingly plump bundle of warmth, the kind of cheerful person who could make a grouch feel loved. Her blond hair was cut in a short, carefree style. "How are your folks, Andi? I worked with your mother years ago at the county fair. She had so many good ideas. We're still using some of them."

"They're doing fine. Dad retired from the oil company a couple of years ago, and they bought a place down at Lake Buchanan. They went to Europe last year. They've been in Australia for the past month and are going to New Zealand next week. Dad told me last night that he was thinking about taking a boat trip from New Zealand to Antarctica. Mom said he was welcome to it; just thinking about it made her cold."

Della shivered. "Me, too. I gripe like the dickens during our summer heat, but if I had to choose, I'd rather be too warm than too cold."

"We'd better be going," said Wade, with a smile. "I want to show Andi around the ranch and let her get some fresh air before she tires out."

"It was so nice to meet you. I've really enjoyed visiting with you," said Andi.

"We enjoyed it, too. You come back anytime you want, whether Wade is around or not. The door's always open. We won't even make you sing for your supper, although we'd let you if you wanted to."

"I haven't done much singing lately, but I expect that will change before long. Thanks for the iced tea and cookies. They were delicious."

"Old family recipe," said Ray.

Della laughed. "Right off the chocolate chip package."

Wade caught Andi's hand. "Come on, woman, the day's gettin' away from us." He slipped his arm around her shoulders as they walked to the car. "Are you getting tired?"

"I'm fine." That wasn't exactly an accurate description of the way she felt, but it would have to do. The fact that he had his arm around her shouldn't have been any big deal. But it was. His nearness, his warmth and strength, and the light, tangy fragrance of his after-shave were playing havoc with her senses. Maybe it had something to do with the way he gently caressed her arm, or the way he looked at her—his eyes filled with tenderness, a tiny frown of concern touching his brow.

"Are you sure you feel up to riding around the ranch?"

"I'm sure. I want to see some of those baby critters you were telling me about."

"That should be easy." He smiled and opened the car door

for her before jogging around to the other side.

They stopped by the corrals first. The tiny ponies were still skittish, so they watched their antics from atop the wooden fence. The colt scampered back and forth in front of the little filly, showing off.

"Will you keep them?"

"Probably, although we have sold some for pleasure riding or cutting. Showing cutting horses has become a popular family sport, and we've had several talented animals."

"Don't you use them here on the ranch?"

"Yes, but we have enough. We haven't raised any champions, but they're fine for folks just starting out. I have a friend who helps me work with them. He's not a professional trainer, but he has a real knack with horses." He jumped off the fence, then turned and lifted her down.

"I met Grant on the rodeo circuit. He was one of the best bull riders I've ever seen. He was two rodeos away from winning the World Championship when he drew a bull named Disaster. And in Grant's case, it was. The bull came out of the chute, spun around, and fell over sideways on Grant's leg. Disaster got up, but Grant couldn't. That monster just about finished him off before anybody could help him." He paused, sadness lingering in his eyes. "He never went back to the rodeo."

"How is he now?"

"His knee still bothers him, and he limps sometimes, but he's not one to complain. Thankfully, he had no lasting problems from the other injuries. He has a place south of here, part of a ranch his family used to own. His father lost it about the time Grant started high school, and they moved down near Austin. He saved everything he could when he was in the rodeo and bought back part of the land. He's determined to get back the rest."

On the way to his house, they passed the two smaller houses where the ranch hands lived.

"How many cowboys do you have?"

"Three. The two single men share a place. The other man is married and has two kids." He motioned to the yard containing a swing set. "Easy to figure out which house is theirs."

Wade's home, a large, red brick rambler, was about a hundred yards farther down the road around a curve. As they approached it, Andi studied him out of the corner of her eye. "Why do I get the feeling that you're troubled because Grant is trying to buy back his land?"

"He's obsessed with it. I'm afraid he will wake up one day and realize he let life pass him by. He might have the land but be all alone, with no one to enjoy it with him."

"What about you? Do you ever think about getting married?"

He glanced at her, but she was gazing out the window, as if only mildly interested in his answer. *All the time since you came home. If things were different....* "I'd like to get married someday and have a couple of kids, but I'm in no rush. How about you?"

She turned, meeting his gaze. For an instant, he saw stark loneliness in her eyes, then her expression changed as she tried to hide her feelings. He heard a trace of wistfulness in her voice when she answered. "I think about it sometimes. I'm not sure I could handle marriage and my career. Some folks do it, but a lot of them don't. The last thing I want is to make a promise I can't keep." She looked back down the road. "The music business is hard on marriages."

"Any career can be, if it's all consuming. That's what happened to my folks." He pulled the roadster up beside the house, parking next to his mud-splattered pickup.

"Being a doctor must make it difficult to have a normal family life." She didn't wait for him to go around and open the door but hopped out and met him at the back of the car.

"Not so much in our case. Dad is an orthopedic surgeon, so most of his time at the office or the hospital was scheduled during the day. There were occasional emergencies in the middle of the night, but it didn't happen too often.

"Mother is an assistant district attorney in Dallas. She is very good at her job, which in itself is fine. Unfortunately, her career means more to her than anything else. Always has."

"And it still hurts."

He shrugged. "Sometimes. Every time I ask the Lord to help me not feel bitterness toward her, something happens to stir it all up again. I'm working on it, but I don't seem to get very far. I've finally decided to handle our relationship the way she's wanted all along. I don't bother her. I don't call, or write, or visit. If she needs to get in touch with me, she knows where to find me."

"How long has it been?"

"Close to a year."

The dark shadow passing over his face told her that she had stirred up a painful memory. "I'm sorry. I shouldn't have pried."

"Don't worry about it. You can leave your purse in the house if you want." He smiled. "It won't matter out here if your hair gets windblown."

She smiled back and walked up onto the porch, which ran the width of the house. An inviting, old fashioned, white swing with a green cushion hung from the rafters of the porch. When they stepped inside, Andi glanced around in approval. The whole front of the house was one large open space, containing a country style kitchen, dining area, and living room. It was definitely a man's home—not a doily or frilly pillow in sight. The soft brown leather sofa and chairs were trimmed in oak, matching the heavy oak coffee table and end tables.

She laid her purse on the coffee table and smiled to herself, remembering her mental image of Wade watching cartoons. More than likely, he had been lying back in his huge leather recliner. The chair sat at an angle so he could see the television or look out the large picture window that framed a spectacular view of the valley and the hills in the distance.

One wall held the television, stereo, and floor-to-ceiling book-shelves, overflowing with reading material of all kinds. A black cast-iron wood stove with a glass door sat in one corner of the room. Andi closed her eyes, imagining how nice it would be to sit snuggled up to him on a cold winter night and watch the flames dancing in a crackling fire.

She felt his arm go around her waist and his warm breath on her ear as he asked softly, "Darlin', are you all right?"

A little thrill spiraled through her. *Don't get so excited about a simple endearment—one cowboys use all the time.* But it didn't seem simple. The way he said the word made it seem very important. She rested her temple against his jaw. "I'm fine. I was imagining a warm, cozy fire on a cold winter night." She leaned back so she could look at him. "That's a bad habit I have, closing my eyes when I'm trying to picture something, or when I'm grasping for the right words to a song."

He grinned and stepped back. "Hope you don't do that when you're driving."

She snapped her fingers. "That's why the guy behind me

always honks when the light turns green."

"Or maybe he wants an autograph." Putting both hands on her upper arms, he steered her toward the door. "I'll show you the rest of the house later. The sunshine won't wait."

As he slowly drove down the dirt road separating the pasture from the fields, Andi admitted she knew very little about ranching. "I know you raise beef cattle, and that the black ones are Angus and the red ones with the white faces are Herefords, but that's about it."

He shook his head and smiled. "How can you claim to be a Texas gal and be so ignorant?"

"Because this Texas gal grew up in town, and my daddy was an oil man. Now, ask me about rigs, wells, or the current price of Texas crude, and I can talk for an hour. I can also spout off about vegetable gardens and thirty different kinds of roses, but I can't tell you much about the native vegetation. When I was a kid, I wasn't interested in such things."

"Didn't your friend Becky live in the country?"

"Yes, but boys were all we ever talked about."

He chuckled. "That doesn't surprise me. You had your pick of the litter."

"You make it sound as if we were choosing pets."

"Weren't you? Half the guys in school had a crush on one or both of you. Let's see. What was that old song? Something about puppy love..." He grinned at her, mischief twinkling in his eyes. "No wonder you changed boyfriends like most people changed socks. All that panting and drooling and gettin' licked in the face."

She playfully smacked him on the shoulder. Laughing, he

dodged and almost drove over a stump. "Keep it in the road, Jamison. And nobody licked me in the face."

Andi pointed to a leafless, rough barked tree with long thorns sprinkled along the branches. "I do know a mesquite when I see one. Grandma said you could tell spring had really arrived when the mesquites started to put out leaves. That's prickly pear cactus over there."

"Both of which are good cattle feed."

She frowned and curled one leg up on the seat, facing him. "They're both covered with thorns."

"Pretty observant for a town girl. The cattle eat the mesquite beans when they ripen and drop from the tree. In dry years, we burn the thorns off the prickly pear with a propane flame thrower so the cattle can eat the pads. They think they're gettin' a special treat. The wife of one of our hired hands picks the pads when they are young and tender, peals off the skin and thorns, and fries them. He says they're real tasty, but I haven't tried them. Aunt Della sometimes makes prickly pear jelly from the fruit. It's good.

"There are some ranchers who actually plant the cactus as feed for their cattle. Still others are developing spineless varieties. Some folks think the fruit and pads will be a hot produce item. They want to call them cactus pears instead of prickly pears because it sounds a little friendlier," he said with a smile.

He continued down the dirt road, stopping whenever she spied something of interest, whether it was a flower or a newborn calf or the crop growing in the field.

"That's winter wheat. We plant it in the fall and let the cattle graze on it during the winter. We have more wheat in other areas of the ranch and rotate the cows between it and the pasture. We also supplement the grain and grass with protein feed from the store. They're finished in the wheat now. We let it grow, and if it heads out, we harvest it and sell it. If there isn't enough rain for it to head out, we'll just plow it under."

"What will be here?" Andi pointed to the bare, plowed dirt in the second field as they drove by.

"Sudan, a kind of sorghum grass. We'll plant here and in several other fields next month. If we put the cattle in to graze too soon, they get sick, but once it's high enough, they can stay until frost. Some of the Sudan is reserved for hay, so the cows don't dine there—unless they knock down the fence and help themselves. Let's go over to the water tank. We should be able to see more cattle there."

He pulled off the road into the pasture, driving around more mesquite trees and prickly pear cactus, bouncing over bumps and across dips and shallow gullies. A few minutes later, he stopped by a large, bowl-shaped, earthen water hole. The tank, which obviously had been dug out with a bulldozer, was about thirty feet in diameter. Two white-faced, red Herefords stood in the edge of the water, about three feet down the sloping bank from the top. The animals raised their heads, staring at them. Another Hereford, accompanied by a shy reddish-brown calf meandered toward the truck. "I'll see if I can get more to drop by for a visit."

Andi jumped when Wade honked the horn. As he continued to honk, cows of varying sizes came toward them from all directions, some walking, some running, a few calling out a noisy welcome. Most of the full-grown cows walked, many followed by little calves. Some of the younger cows acted like teenagers, racing each other across the pasture. One bumped into another one, shoving it aside, and rushed ahead of the others. "They love you so much, all you have to do is whistle...uh, I mean honk?"

Wade sighed dramatically, but his eyes sparkled. "Sadly, it's not me they love. They think I'm going to feed them."

"But you're not?"

"Not this time. We put out a load of feed a couple of days ago. They have plenty of grass now, so that will have to do. Feed is expensive."

"Tricking them like this seems kind of mean."

"I suppose it is, but it's a good way to check the herd, which has to be done even when we aren't feeding them store-bought food."

"Don't cowboys roundup anymore?"

"Sure we do. Every spring and fall. Some ranches use helicopters for the brush work. We still like to do it the old fashioned way—on horseback. Roundups are for branding and other stuff that only gets done once or twice a year. A rancher keeps a close eye on his herd, checking them every day if he can, keeping a count to make sure they are all here. The hired hands check on them and take a count, too, whenever they are working in a particular area."

He pulled a small spiral notebook from his shirt pocket. "This is one of the best record keeping systems ever devised. I don't know when it started, but ranchers were using it at the beginning of this century. We note the number and type of cattle in each field or pasture, then count them whenever we can. There should be thirty-five head in this pasture, but we might not see them all here at the tank. Some may be resting in the shade or down by the creek.

"A cattleman watches how the little ones are growing, how fat the big ones are getting, whether any of them are sick, or if they've knocked down a fence and wandered into the neighbor's pasture. Sometimes, by calling the cows up like this, we do a good deed. See that little brown calf?"

"Which one?" Andi sat up straight, stretching to see out his window. There were three calves of varying shades of brown on that side of the truck.

"The one that's making such a racket." He nudged his hat up off his forehead. "Scoot over this way." When she slid across the seat, he put his arm around her and pulled her up next to him. "I never realized looking at livestock could be this much fun," he murmured.

"Me, either. Maybe I should have dated more country boys," she said with a teasing grin. A pathetic, high pitched bawling near the truck drew her attention. Andi leaned toward the window, resting one arm against Wade's chest and the other on the steering wheel, and looked out at brown calf number four. "Oh, the poor baby. He looks so unhappy."

"He's hungry. His mama probably left him with a baby-sitter, and he got to playing with some of his friends and went off with them when their mamas came back."

"A baby-sitter?" She glanced at him, unsure of whether or not he was teasing.

"They take turns. It's not uncommon to see five or six calves playing around one lone cow while the others are off grazing or getting a drink. Seems like they basically take the duty a day at a time. That's his mother over there." He pointed to a cow trotting through a maze of mesquite trees.

"How do you know that's his mother? A lot of them look the same to me."

"When you're around them all the time, you notice details that distinguish each one from the others. See that small pear shaped white spot on her shoulder?" At her nod, he continued, "I was here Monday morning right after she gave birth to the light brown calf with the white patch on his forehead."

They watched the happy reunion between hungry baby and worried mother. As Andi settled back against the cushion, Wade moved his arm, resting it across the top of the seat. She sensed that he didn't want her to move to the other side of the truck, but that he wouldn't say anything if she did. She stayed where she was.

She pointed to another calf with coloring almost identical to the one that had been separated from its mother. "You knew that calf wasn't hers because it's bigger and its coat is a little bit darker brown?"

"The lady learns fast. That calf was born two weeks ago. His mama is the big one over there with one twisted horn." He pointed to a cow a short distance in front of them. "She's older than we are."

"You're kidding."

"Nope. Uncle Ray says she's thirty years old. She had her first calf about the time we were born and has had one a year ever since. This one has more than earned her keep and a lazy retirement." A loud bellow sounded nearby on the right, and Andi jumped. Wade slid his arm down from the seat, resting it across her shoulders. "That's the big guy making his grand entrance."

Andi watched a gigantic, reddish-brown bull strut into view. "He's beautiful."

"Handsome brute, that's a fact. Uncle Ray used to raise purebred Herefords, but he bought a couple of Beefmaster bulls several years back as an experiment. They improved the quality of the herd, so he switched mainly to Beefmaster bulls and Hereford

67

cows. We breed the heifers who haven't had a calf with Longhorns. The calf is smaller and makes it easier on first-time mothers."

"Will we see a Longhorn?"

"Not in this pasture. We have to keep them well separated from the other bulls, or they tear them up. In fact, we've had to shorten the horns on a couple of them. Hated to do it. Cutting off their horns takes away their pride, but it keeps them out of fights. We'll go see if we can find one."

He lifted his arm over her head, putting his hand back on the steering wheel. "Feel free to stay where you are," he said with a warm, roguish smile.

Andi laughed softly as he drove past the tank, feeling free for the first time in years. Sitting close to him was like coming home, and at that moment, she didn't ever want to leave again.

Six

❧

ndi and Wade sat on the grassy bank beside one of the three creeks that cut across the ranch, basking in the sunshine, enjoying the peace and quiet. A hawk soared high overhead in lazy circles. A dragonfly flew past, and on the opposite bank, a woodpecker hammered away, looking for lunch in the side of a mesquite tree.

Their trip to see the Longhorn had been a success. Andi was duly impressed with the six feet span of horns, but the thought of Wade working with the potentially dangerous animal frightened her. He had driven past the fifteen acre garden which supplied vegetables for his family as well as those who worked on the ranch. She knew from experience that a garden could take up a lot of space if watermelons and cantaloupes were planted in it, but it was still the largest garden plot she had ever seen, short of a commercial one.

She leaned back on her elbows, watching the hawk. "I've heard you should never ask a rancher how big his spread is or how many cows he has because that's like asking him how much money he makes."

"True." Wade glanced at her and grinned. "But you still want to know, don't you?"

"I'm not interested in how much money you make, but I am curious about how big this place is. It seems like we drove twenty miles today."

He laughed. "You have to remember we back-tracked a lot. We have close to twenty-five thousand acres, which equals thirty-nine sections or thirty-nine square miles."

She whistled softly. "Not too shabby."

"There are bigger ranches around, but we're doing all right. Aunt Della's grandfather started the ranch. Each generation has added to it." He glanced up at the position of the sun. "We'd better head back. It will start cooling off soon, and we have quite a little hike to the pickup."

They walked along the dry portion of the sandy, occasionally rocky, creek bed in silence, listening to the bubbling music of the shallow stream that flowed beside them. Tall, bright green grass grew along the banks near the water, with mesquites and weeping willows for a backdrop. Andi didn't think she had ever been in such a tranquil place. Nature's hushed sounds seeped into her soul, giving her a momentary sense of peace.

They were halfway back to the pickup when weariness began to settle over her. She didn't say anything and fought the fatigue, hoping that complete exhaustion wouldn't hit her. For most of the afternoon, she had forgotten about being in the recovery stages of a serious illness. She had felt almost normal, relaxed and happier than she had been in ages. Angrily, she silently railed against her unwanted limitations.

When they reached a narrow point where they could jump across the stream, she decided to take off her shoes in case she couldn't make it. She tossed them over the water to the other side.

He stopped with a frown. "You aren't thinking about wading across, are you?"

"No, but I'm not sure I can jump that far. It looks wider than when we crossed earlier."

Wade raised one eyebrow. "It's not." He slid his arm around her back, supporting her weight, and frowned again. "Andi, why didn't you tell me you're getting tired? You're trembling."

Before she realized his intention, he had swung her up in his arms. "Wade, you don't have to carry me. I just need to rest a minute. I'll be okay."

"Quiet, woman," he said sternly, then softened his command with a smile. "Relax and enjoy it. I'm going to."

Andi laughed and put her arms around his neck. "If you want to act macho, I won't stop you. You do it so well."

He winked. "And don't you forget it." Clearing the water with one long step, he lowered her feet to the ground, so she could pick up her shoes. Then he picked her up again and quickly covered the remaining distance with his easy stride.

Andi felt a twinge of regret when they reached the pickup, and he gently set her feet on the ground. "Thanks. I hate to admit it, but I'm worn out."

"You should have said something." He opened the pickup door, put his hands to her waist, and lifted her up on the seat.

"You're right, but it irritates the life out of me to give in to it."

"I do believe you're as stubborn as you are pretty."

How was she supposed to respond to that one? She decided not to even try. Instead, she slumped down, resting her head on the back of the seat. "Home, James."

He touched the rim of his hat with his forefinger and thumb. "Yes, ma'am."

When they arrived at his house, he pointed toward the sofa. "You can nap there as long as you like, unless you want me to take you on home."

She was practically falling asleep standing up, but she didn't want to leave. "I might perk up if I rest awhile." She paused by the back door, slipped off her sandy shoes, and went straight to the sofa. He stopped, too, using a cast-iron bootjack to remove his boots, then brought her a heavy afghan, pillow, and a cold glass of water.

After taking a long drink, she lay down on the sofa. Wade was at her side in an instant, pulling the afghan up over her, tucking it around her shoulders and under her chin. "You'll make a good daddy," she murmured.

A strange, deep sadness filled his eyes. "I hope I get the chance someday." He brushed her cheek with his knuckle. "Have a good rest, songbird."

For the next two hours, Wade relaxed in his recliner and watched her sleep, memorizing the contours of her face, the subtle changes of expression as she dreamed. Spending the afternoon with her had been a mistake in some ways. His love had grown with every passing hour, with each sunlit smile and golden laugh. In those brief moments when she revealed her sadness or showed weakness, the tenderness and protectiveness he felt had almost overwhelmed him. The more he was with her, the harder it would be when she left, yet he would greedily claim every second they could be together, storing up treasures to last a lifetime.

"I want what I can't have, Lord," he whispered. "Help me not to cross the line." As darkness fell, the room grew chilled. He built a fire in the wood stove and turned on a lamp. A short time later Andi began to stir, so he went into the kitchen, heated some soup, and made sandwiches.

When he carried the food in on a tray and set it on the coffee table, she sat up and ran her hand through her disheveled hair. Still groggy, she stared at him and blinked her big brown eyes like a sleepy owl. It was all he could do to keep from taking her into his arms. "Hi, sleepyhead. Want some supper?"

"Umph." She scratched her head and wrinkled up her face, then yawned and stretched. "Guess so. What is it?"

He chuckled. "Didn't know you were so picky. Ham and cheese sandwiches and vegetable beef soup. The canned kind. Nothing I can mess up."

"Sounds good." She looked out the window at the darkness. "How long did I sleep?"

"Couple of hours." He sat down beside her.

"That's me. Life of the party," she said with a grimace.

"I didn't mind. I rested awhile and got some stuff done." He hoped she didn't ask what. He wasn't sure she would consider watching her as "doing stuff," or if she would be comfortable with it.

"Shall we ask the blessing?" When he held out his hand, she took it and bowed her head. He thanked the Lord for the food and the day they had spent together. After the prayer, he picked up half of a sandwich. "Did you see TNN 'Country News' last night?" She shook her head. "I missed it, too, but taped it. Do you want to watch it and see what's going on with your cohorts?" he asked.

"Sure. They have some good reports." She began eating her

soup as he turned on the television with the remote and switched the channel to The Nashville Network.

The first report, about the making of a new music video by a leading male vocalist, was followed by an interview with a singer who had a secondary role in a Western movie. Another new star had sold a million copies of his first album, and his record company surprised him with a new Harley Davidson motorcycle.

"The other day a record company gave a guy a new boat. Do they do things like that for everybody?" Wade asked when the program broke for a commercial.

"There is a lot of competition between labels, so they try to keep their performers happy, at least the ones who are doing well. They threw a big party when my second album went platinum and furnished my bedroom and the bathroom on my new bus, right down to gold plated fixtures for the sink and shower." She laughed when Wade choked on a spoonful of soup, then pounded him on the back. "Well, I'm not into motorcycles or boats, so they had to come up with something."

The program returned, and an incredibly beautiful picture of Andi flashed on the screen. Wade caught his breath. It was a publicity shot, elegant in its simplicity. Her dark hair was parted in the center and curved gracefully along her jaw line. She wore a black sweater with a loose cowl collar which exposed the base of her neck and throat. Her faint smile teased the viewer with a hint of her dimples, but her large eyes were dark and mysterious.

"Although singer Andi Carson is recuperating from her bout with pneumonia and anemia in an undisclosed location," said the pretty female broadcaster, "her agent, Kyle Wilson, head of KW Entertainment, told us get well wishes and gifts have been pouring in since she collapsed during a performance in Tucson, Arizona."

The scene changed to an office reception area overflowing with boxes of letters and gifts. A reporter held out the microphone to a man in his early to mid-thirties who looked like a soap opera heart throb. Wade knew it was wrong, but he detested Kyle on sight, and only partly because the man worked Andi too hard.

"The outpouring of love from Andi's fans has been overwhelming," said Kyle. "I talked to her this morning, and she's feeling stronger day by day. We've sent some mail to her already and will be sending all of these letters and gifts out tonight. I know they will boost her spirits and hasten her recovery."

"Do you have any idea when Andi will return to work?" asked the reporter.

"As soon as her doctor gives his approval. We're hoping to have that in a couple of weeks, but of course, we don't want her to go back to work until she is completely well. When he gives us the go-ahead, we'll firm up the new dates for the shows we had to cancel. Andi doesn't want to disappoint any of her fans. That's why she tried to do the show in Tucson even though she was very ill. She loves them as much as they love her."

The scene switched back to the broadcaster. "We would also like to extend our wishes for a quick recovery to Andi. She's a lady who gives her all to her music and her fans and is destined to go to great heights in the country music industry. We look forward to having you back, Andi."

Stunned, Wade turned off the television. He'd had no idea she had collapsed during a performance. She should have been in a hospital long before she set foot on that stage. Even his mother, as driven as she was to succeed, would have chosen her health over her job.

The sheer volume of letters and gifts left him speechless, partly because he suddenly realized they came from a small portion of her fans. Whenever he thought about her albums selling a million copies, he had envisioned stacks and stacks of CDs and cassettes. He had not tried to imagine the number in terms of people.

The broadcaster's words about Andi's devotion to her music and her fans and being destined for greatness rang in his ears. None of that was news to him. Then why did having those beliefs confirmed make him feel as if he had fallen into a bottomless pit?

Trying to deal with the barrage of emotions, Wade did not think about Andi's reaction to the story until she slowly got up and walked over to the front window. He turned off the lamp and joined her. Moonlight draped the valley in silver, and thousands of stars sparkled in the dark heavens. Nearby, an owl hooted, and in the distance, an elusive pack of coyotes howled and yipped in excited communication.

He glanced at Andi. She stood with her back straight, her arms crossed in front of her like a shield. He shoved his hands into the pockets of his jeans. "You didn't tell me you collapsed on stage," he said quietly.

"Didn't I? I guess I never thought to mention it." She kept her gaze fixed on the landscape.

"Why did you try to perform that night? Why didn't you go to a doctor?"

"I had seen a doctor earlier in the week. He gave me some antibiotics and cough medicine and told me to rest. We had two days without a concert, so I took my medicine and practically slept around the clock. I woke up at four o'clock the next afternoon in Tucson and felt terrible, but it was too late to cancel the show outright. Those people had spent their hard-earned money on tickets to see me, and I had an obligation to them. Some had driven over a hundred miles, and I didn't have the heart to let them down.

"By the time I stepped on stage, I knew I'd made a big mistake. I was so weak I could hardly stand up and had to sit on a stool. I felt as if a giant was standing on my chest and stabbing me every time I took a breath.

"I told the audience that I wasn't feeling well, and that we were going to do a couple of songs as a thank you for coming and refund their money. I almost made it through the first song before I passed out."

"So Kyle didn't push you to do the show?"

"No. He told me to do whatever I needed to do. He was in Los Angeles so he couldn't see how bad I was. Unfortunately, I wasn't in any shape to make a coherent decision. I'd been too tired to think straight for over a month.

"He took the first flight out of Los Angeles when he heard I was in the hospital. I didn't wake up until late the next day, and he was there in my room, napping in a chair. I'd never been in a hospital. I don't know what I would have done without him."

Wade's low opinion of the man raised considerably, even as his jealousy increased.

"I was on oxygen, hooked up to I don't know how many monitors, and had all these tubes poking in me. I was so scared." The sleeve of her sweater brushed against his arm when she shuddered.

With only the moonlight and the soft, flickering light from the fire surrounding them, it seemed natural to step behind her and put his arms around her. He rested his cheek against her soft, fragrant hair and closed his eyes.

She tensed, then relaxed, and covered his hands with hers. "They had trouble contacting my folks because they were on a trek across the Australian outback. By the time Kyle reached them, we knew I would be all right, so I told them not to come home. Dawn flew in to keep me company. Kyle needed to be in Los Angeles, so he left when she got there. He'd already sent the band and road crew home."

"I'm glad Dawn was there." He tried to lighten her spirits. "If I'd known, I would have sent you flowers or maybe a giant bunch of balloons."

"That would have been sweet, although I don't know where we would have put them. They wouldn't let me have any flowers in the room at first. Later, there were so many, I wound up having Dawn take them to other patients."

"A lot of people love you." Without thinking, he tightened his arms.

"I know they do, and I appreciate it. I love them, too, in many ways."

"But?"

She took a deep breath, releasing it slowly. "I don't know if I can explain it."

"Take your time. I'm not going anywhere."

She hesitated and her fingers pressed harder against his hands. "There are people who like my music, and some who care for me as a person, but I'm still lonely. I have been for a long time. I walk out on stage and the audience goes nuts. It pleases me to know they enjoy my music, but deep inside I feel so cold, so empty. When I'm with my family or friends, it's a little better, but there is still something missing." She turned in his arms, facing him, resting her hands against his chest. "I don't want to be alone anymore. I don't know if I can stand it."

Heart pounding, Wade looked down into her dark eyes, aching at the despair he saw there. Words of love sprang up in his heart, promises he barely kept from tumbling from his lips. Nothing on earth could keep him from lowering his head toward hers and try to take away her hurt in the gentleness of his kiss.

He rejoiced as she welcomed him, accepting his tenderness as a soothing balm. Then without warning, in spite of his hard won restraint, the kiss took on a new urgency, a deeper fervor, as she sought more than solace.

Sensing her desperation, he reluctantly raised his head and cradled her tenderly against him. She cared for him; he felt it in her touch. But she didn't love him—not with the last-a-lifetime kind of love he had to have.

And it was just as well. He could never be the kind of man she needed, traveling with the rodeo had taught him that. He needed to be on the ranch, working in the open country, not constantly moving from city to city. Trying to adapt to her lifestyle would be tantamount to throwing a rope around his neck and tightening the loop a little more each day until he suffocated.

"I'd better go home." She pushed lightly on his chest and he released her. She shoved her hair back out of her face, revealing her flushed cheeks. "I'm sorry. I didn't mean to come on to you like that. I know what you must think."

Honey, you don't have a clue. "What?" He followed her toward the back door, blinking as she switched on the kitchen light.

"That I've…that I've probably been with lots of men." She pulled on one shoe. "Let's face it. Entertainers aren't often perceived as having very good morals." She put on the other shoe, then straightened.

Wade tugged on his second boot, practically holding his breath to see where the conversation was going. He wasn't sure he really wanted to know. He straightened and looked at her. "Some of them do."

"And some of them don't. It's not unusual for one or two of my band members to down a six-pack and go find a wife for the night. We have groupies that follow us from town to town." She twisted a strand of hair around her finger.

He leaned against the kitchen counter. "Do any men follow you?"

"Some have, but it didn't do them any good." She pulled her finger loose from the loop of hair and looked down, rubbing a smudge on the vinyl floor with the toe of her shoe.

He had the feeling she wished she hadn't said anything. He gently nudged her chin up with his knuckle. "Andi, what are you trying to tell me?"

She met his gaze and took a deep breath. "That I'm not like those guys in the band, in spite of the way I acted a few minutes ago. When I get married and make love to my husband, it will be my first time."

Hallelujah! He pushed away from the counter and slowly framed her face with both hands.

Mesmerized, Andi stared up at him, holding her breath. His eyes glowed softly with tenderness and admiration, but something else danced in the shadows, flitting into the light for a heartbeat before it was hidden again. Something so beautiful she dared not give it a name. Then his lips touched hers in a whisper kiss, and pure sweetness filled her soul. He raised his head and brushed her cheeks with his thumbs before dropping his hands to his sides. "What was that?" she whispered.

"Man thanking woman for a precious gift." He gave her a lopsided grin. "You're right. I'd better take you home. I'm starting to wax poetic and that could get bad."

She smiled. "I don't know, I kinda like it."

They drove back to town, listening to the radio, sometimes singing along, simply enjoying each other's company. By the time they strolled up the front steps of Dawn's house, he knew there was something he was supposed to say. He felt awkward, considering that in high school, she had been the one talking to him about walking with Jesus.

A policeman drove past, tossing them a wave and a grin. Wade glanced up at the bright porch light and decided talking was all he could do. It was too well lighted and too public to even think about a lingering good night kiss.

"You have a wonderful ranch. Thank you for such a nice day." Andi smiled up at him.

"I enjoyed it, too. Maybe you can come out again before long."

"I'd like that."

He opened the screen door. As she reached for the doorknob on the front door, he laid his hand on her shoulder. She looked up at him, her expression questioning. "You really aren't alone, you know. Jesus is walking right beside you."

She shook her head. "I don't think so. I'm afraid I strayed off the path a long time ago."

"It doesn't matter. Remember his promise? 'Never will I leave you; never will I forsake you.' "

"But what if we leave him?" she whispered. "What if we forsake him?"

81

"Romans says that nothing can separate us from the love of God that is in Christ Jesus our Lord. Not death or life, angels or demons, the present or the future, any powers, height or depth or anything in all creation will be able to separate us from his love. If you reach out to him, you'll find that he's right there waiting for you."

She was still clearly troubled, unconvinced.

"Think about it. That's all I'm asking. You're his child, and he loves you very much." He smiled and tucked a strand of hair behind her ear. "Ten years ago, you told me to put my hand in his, to trust him with my hurt and my problems. I'm kinda hard-headed, so it took a few years before I followed your advice. Others shared his love and nurtured me, but you planted the seeds, Andi. It was remembering your belief in him, your faith and trust, that kept me from turning my back on him completely. I never did thank you for that," he said thoughtfully.

"You just did." She tried to smile, but it wobbled around the edges.

"I guess so." He smiled and glanced up and down the street. Not a car in sight, and it looked as if the neighbors weren't home. He dropped a quick kiss on her cheek, then opened the front door. "I'll give you a call tomorrow. Sleep well."

"Yeah, right." She shook her head, but her smile held firm. "Since I got sick, my poor brain has cranked out some pretty weird dreams. After all that has happened today and everything we've talked about, they're bound to be doozies."

"That's probably where some movie makers get their ideas. You could start a whole new career."

She laughed and poked him in the stomach with her finger. "Say good night, Wade."

" 'Good night, Wade.' "

Groaning at his corny joke, she tried to poke him again, but he jumped out of the way with a laugh.

He stopped at the edge of the porch, one foot on the first step, and looked back at her. "Good night, darlin'."

He kept his smile until she went inside and closed the door. Walking to the Blazer, he whistled an old, mournful cowboy tune, wishing with all his heart for what could never be.

Seven

Andi went inside and closed the front door behind her. Pausing for a moment, she listened to the tune Wade was whistling, an old song of unrequited love. Hearing those sad notes confirmed her belief that what he felt for her went beyond friendship and physical attraction. She wondered if over time, it could grow into love.

Is there a future for us? The depth of her hope and longing frightened her. Could she be imagining her feelings for him simply because she wanted so badly to care for someone and have him care for her? The last thing in the world she wanted was to hurt him. He was tender, considerate, and protective. Maybe too protective. She was used to fending for herself against the often overwhelming demands placed on her. It would be easy to grow too dependent upon him.

Dawn looked up from the romance novel she was reading, interrogating her cousin with her gaze. "Well?"

Andi dropped into the big, comfortable, yellow chair. "I like him a lot. And he likes me. Maybe a lot. I think I can safely say we've moved a step beyond merely being friends."

"So I assume he kissed you?"

Andi laughed softly. Her cousin could be the most tactful person on earth when she wanted to be, or the most direct. "Nosy. Yes, he kissed me."

"And?"

"And what?" She couldn't resist teasing her.

"What was it like? Did you hear a symphony?"

Andi considered the question, remembering those precious moments. "No symphony, but a flute, the sweetest, purest notes drifting on the wind."

Dawn sighed. "How romantic."

"And fireworks. Big time. Like the Fourth of July at the Statue of Liberty."

Dawn's golden brown eyes grew wide. "Oh, my." She groaned and pounded her fist on the couch. "I'm green with envy. I don't think I'm ever going to find the right man. Not in this one-horse town, anyway."

"I thought you liked living here."

"I do. I wouldn't really want to live anywhere else. But I think I've dated every eligible man within twenty miles—except Wade. I haven't had fireworks with anybody. Haven't even heard a fire-cracker or a sparkler."

Andi laughed. "Sparklers don't make noise."

"Sometimes they kind of sputter." Dawn made a face. "Guess I wouldn't want a man who sputtered anyway." Her expression grew solemn. "I've had a few offers. Maybe I'm being too picky."

"No, you're not. You'd be miserable if you married someone you didn't love."

"True." Dawn smiled, her eyes sparkling. "What about you

86

and Wade? Think this is going somewhere?"

"I don't know. I'd like it to, but I don't think he could stand to be away from the ranch for long. It wouldn't be fair to ask him to leave it and go on tour with me. Plus there are recording sessions in Nashville and publicity appearances and video sessions.... There is hardly a free day."

"Maybe you could cut down a little and space things out so you could be home more."

"Maybe, but I'm not sure I want a week-or-two-a-month marriage. I don't know if I could manage both a career and a successful marriage. It scares me to think about it." She sighed heavily and hugged a fat throw pillow to her chest. "Right now, I could care less if I ever perform again."

Dawn stared at her, shocked. "You can't be serious. That's all you've ever wanted. All you've worked for since you were in high school. Andi, you're a star. You've made it. Millions of people love to hear you sing."

"It has its moments, but believe me, it ain't all it's made out to be." She lowered the pillow to her lap, crushing the edges with her hands. "I know I sound like an ungrateful brat, but how much gratitude do I owe my fans? How long must I be responsible for Kyle and all the others who work for me? Do I owe them all so much that I have to sacrifice what I want more than anything?"

"No, you don't," said Dawn quietly, beginning to understand the depth of Andi's conflict and unhappiness. "What do you want more than anything?"

"A husband, children, and a loving home where we're all together."

"It seems to me you have a big decision to make. Have you

talked to God about it?" Dawn knew she was treading on unsettled ground. She was well aware that her cousin hadn't been to church in years, that somewhere along the way, she had quit trusting in God to guide her.

"You sound like Wade. The way you two talk, all I have to do is turn my life over to God and all my troubles will be solved instantly." Andi frowned and threw the pillow on the floor.

"They might be. Or it might take a long time. Sometimes things happen because God wants us to change or has something he wants us to learn. All I'm saying is that when you make Jesus a part of your life, you have someone to talk to, someone to guide you. He's not called Wise Counselor just because it sounds nice."

"He doesn't seem to have solved all of your problems." Andi was being sarcastic, even nasty, but she couldn't seem to help it. Relinquishing control of her life was difficult, and in her heart, she knew that's what she would have to do if she turned back to God. She couldn't simply give him lip service and then do her own thing. For her, it was all or nothing.

"No, he hasn't. Not yet, but I do believe he knows what is best for me. And I suppose when it comes to relationships, one person involved might be ready before the other one is. Free will is a part of it, too. God lets us make our own choices, whether they are right or wrong, but when we make the right one, we know it because we have peace."

Peace. Like I felt at the ranch today, thought Andi.

"Of course, human emotions get involved and too often mess things up. Human logic, too. My biggest problem is impatience—not that anyone would notice. That's probably why God is taking forever to let me find my man." She rolled her eyes. "Don't ever ask God to teach you patience. What a bummer!"

Andi smiled in spite of her turbulent emotions. "I'll remember that." She paused, feeling the weariness creep over her again. "I'm afraid I've been a big disappointment to God. I'm not sure he wants me back."

"Are you nuts? Think what a witness you could be. Not that you would have to start preaching or anything, but your life is so visible to so many, just the fact that you love him would make an impact." Dawn's voice grew soft. "And even if you weren't Andi Carson, the big singing star, he would love you. There is room in God's heart and his kingdom for all who seek him, whether great or small, rich or poor, good or bad. Why don't you come to church with me in the morning?"

"I don't know." Andi hedged. "Let me think about it. Check with me in the morning. I've got to hit the sack. I'm zonked and my head aches."

"Okay. See you in the morning." Dawn watched her cousin shuffle off to the bedroom. *Please, dear Lord, give her the courage to commit her life to you again. Let her find direction, peace, and happiness.*

Though her mind was in a turmoil, Andi fell asleep shortly after she went to bed. Her rest was fitful, plagued by crazy, unsettling dreams. When Dawn gently woke her on Sunday morning, she was still exhausted. Her head felt as if a little gremlin was standing inside it beating a sledge hammer against a giant bass drum. She sat up slowly, holding the top of her head.

"You don't look too good." Dawn frowned and felt Andi's forehead. "No temperature, but you're white as a ghost. Headache worse?"

"Awful. I'm afraid I did way too much yesterday."

"How are your lungs?"

Andi took a deep breath. "Clear. I don't need the oxygen bottle." She tried to smile but failed.

"I'll get you something for your headache, then you'd better go back to sleep. Are you hungry?"

Andi's stomach recoiled at the thought of food. "No, but I'd like to sleep for a week."

She slept until late afternoon. She awoke refreshed and without the headache. With her stomach rumbling, she strolled into the kitchen.

Dawn was sitting at the table, balancing her checkbook. "How are you feeling?"

"Normal and hungry. What are you cooking?" Andi sniffed and headed toward the stove. "Smells good."

"Beef and barley soup. It should be done. Help yourself while I clear up this mess."

"You want some?"

"Yes. I have to leave for choir practice in about an hour. Don't want my stomach growling." Dawn cleared off the table while Andi filled the soup bowls and put out some crackers. She poured them each a glass of iced tea and sat down to eat. "Wade asked about you this morning. He was very concerned to hear you weren't feeling well. He said to call him if you felt like it. He didn't want to call and wake you up. If you eat fast, you might catch him before he leaves for church."

"He's in the choir, too?"

"Our main bass. He's the only one who can hit the really low notes. He fills in on baritone if we need him, as long as it doesn't go too high."

"He has a beautiful voice. We were singing along with the

radio some last night on the way back to town."

"Plays the guitar, too."

"A man of many talents." Andi devoured half her soup in a very unladylike manner, then set the bowl aside. "I'll finish this after I talk to Wade."

She grabbed the cordless phone and hurried into the bedroom, dialing as she went.

When he answered and found out it was her, his voice instantly grew warmer and dropped a little deeper. "How are you feeling?"

Like I just snuggled up beside you, she thought with a contented smile. "Much better. Guess I'll have to keep taking it easy for a while longer."

"Gets old, doesn't it? I remember how bored I got when I was laid up after my famous last bull ride. Want some company this evening?"

"Sure. Why don't you come by after church?"

"I could run over after choir practice and pick you up if you want to come to the evening service."

She heard the hopefulness in his voice, although she suspected he was trying to sound casual. "Maybe another time."

"All right. I've got to run, or I'll be late. See you a little after seven."

Andi showered and dried her hair, then dressed in a comfortable purple sweat suit with an oversized top. She was taking the hot rollers from her hair when Dawn stuck her head through the doorway and announced she was leaving. Brushing her hair, Andi stared in the mirror. "Well, kid, you've put this off long enough."

She still wasn't convinced that God would welcome her back with open arms, but she felt she had to at least try to talk to him. Restless, she wandered out into the living room. Spotting a Bible on the bookshelf, she picked it up. The cover was a bit worn, and the pages had been handled many times. It was a New International Version, one with which she was not familiar.

She curled up on the couch, holding the Bible. "Heavenly Father, I walked away from you a long time ago," she whispered. "And I feel bad about it. In spite of my unfaithfulness, you've greatly blessed me, and I'm thankful for all the wonderful things that have happened in my career. I should be happy, but I'm not. In many ways, my life is a mess. I've done things I'm ashamed of and other things that probably weren't all that great, either. But I guess right now, more than anything, I'm scared. Scared you don't want me. Scared you'll turn me away." Tears stung her eyes. "I know I don't have a right to ask, but could you give me some kind of reassurance?"

Heart pounding and mind whirling, she waited in tense silence until she felt the urge to read the Bible. She didn't know where to look. A red ribbon was attached to the spine of the book, its length serving as a marker. Gently lifting the frayed end of ribbon, Andi opened the Bible to the book of Hebrews.

Several passages on both pages were underlined, but the one that caught her eye was Hebrews four, verse sixteen, "Let us then approach the throne of grace with confidence, so that we may receive mercy and find grace to help us in our time of need."

A sob broke from her throat and tears filled her eyes. "Oh, Jesus, I do need your mercy and grace. I need you." It was as if a flood gate had opened. Weeping, and at the same time rejoicing in the answer to her prayer, Andi poured out her heart to her Lord. She wasn't aware of how long she sat there, praising him, asking forgiveness when certain things came to mind, seeking his guidance, and finally, simply sitting in still silence, basking in his love and presence.

She heard a car drive up and quickly blew her nose one last time and put the Bible back on the shelf. A knock sounded at the door as she peeked in a small mirror hanging beside the bookshelf and shook her head. She had never been one to cry prettily.

When Andi opened the door, Wade took one look at her puffy eyes and red nose and stepped into the room, gathering her into his arms. "Sugar, what's wrong?"

She laid her head on his shoulder and sighed in contentment. "Nothing."

"No offense, but you look like you've been crying your heart out. Level with me. What happened?" He ran his hand gently up and down her back.

"God and I have been getting reacquainted."

His hand quit moving. "Oh."

She leaned back against his arms and looked up at him. "Didn't God have to do some housecleaning when you first came to him?"

He smiled gently, beautifully. "Did he ever. The house, the garage, the barn, even a few stalls. I was a real mess. He still has to go through the closets every so often."

She grinned and stepped out of his arms, catching his hand. "No doubt I still have lots of cobwebs and corners that need sweeping, but we've made a good start." She waited until he closed the front door, then led him to the sofa. "You were right. He's always been there. All I had to do was reach out and touch him."

Wade sat down beside her and put his arm around her shoulders. "And I bet you don't feel as lonely or as empty as you did a little while ago."

"No, although he did leave some spaces that need filling. It will be interesting to see how he does it. In the meantime, my life is his. I know with all my heart that he loves me and accepts me, warts and all."

He cupped her chin with his hand, tipping her face this way and that. "I don't see any warts." His eyes began to twinkle as he focused on her red nose. "Just Rudolph."

"You really know how to compliment a girl, don't you?"

"Yes, ma'am. I could kiss it and make it better."

"Think it would help?"

"Sure." He caressed her cheek with his thumb and dropped a tiny kiss on the tip of her nose. "And your eyes. They must hurt, too."

"Terribly." She closed her eyes and waited. She wasn't disappointed.

He touched each lid gently, then murmured, "How about your lips?"

"Yes," she whispered.

His first kiss was tender and sweet. The second, long and lingering. Slowly he raised his head. "This could get addictive."

"Pretty potent stuff." She'd never experienced anything like it.

"And dangerous." He straightened and leaned back against the couch, keeping her nestled against his side. "Oh, I forgot to tell you, Dawn went over to Miss Atkins' house. She's recruited her and Harold for the museum committee. She said she'd be home later, maybe around nine or ten." He shifted slightly so

94

she would be more comfortable. "When do you go back to the doctor?"

"Friday afternoon."

"I'll be going over to Sidell on Friday to pick up some tractor parts that are on order. Want me to take you?"

"Hot date, huh? Which shall we do first? Visit the doctor's office or tour the tractor dealer's?"

"Either one you want. And if you don't get too sassy, I might throw in dinner and a movie."

"Now you're talking. But I need to pick up a rental car, too."

"You can borrow the Blazer. I can do without it for a while. I've got the roadster and the pickup."

"Thanks, but I'd rather get my own. I'd feel bad if you needed it, and I was roaming around someplace. Besides, I think I'm in the mood for something sporty, maybe a red convertible."

He frowned down at her. "You don't have any business going off by yourself, especially in a red convertible. That's no way to keep a low profile." When she started to protest, he stopped her. "The sheriff told me that you need a bodyguard whenever you go out in public. What makes you think it will be any different around here?"

"There won't be any problem in Buckley."

"Probably not, until someone tells a friend that you're here, and that friend tells another, and *that* one can't resist calling the media with a hot tip. Before you know it, you won't be able to step out the front door without people swarming all over you. In fact, if you rent a car, the word is likely to spread like wild fire that you're in the area. It wouldn't take a bright reporter to figure out where you're staying."

"You're right. I'll borrow the Blazer, and I won't go anywhere without a disguise. It usually works well. You can't imagine what sunglasses and a curly blond wig will do."

"Turn you into a Dawn clone?"

She laughed. "Not even close."

"Well, you won't need the wig on Friday."

She reached over and felt his hard biceps. "No, I don't believe so." She doubted that the highest paid bodyguard would protect her the way he would.

The next day, Andi waved goodbye as Dawn drove off to visit a customer, then walked back into the living room, her gaze falling on the piano. Happiness brought a smile to her face as the urge to play the beloved instrument returned. She pulled out the old, three legged piano stool and sat down. Thinking of others whose hands had lovingly touched the black and white pieces of ivory, she folded back the cover that protected the keys and ran her fingers lightly over them, her heart soaring at the rich, velvet tones.

Closing her eyes, she pictured her great-grandmother, Granny Mae, bent and frail, sitting there. At age ninety, she had still been able to play the hymns of her youth from memory, never missing a note. Andi's grandmother played hymns, too, and was pianist at the church for twenty years, but her secret love and passion was the blues. During Andi's visits, they spent much of their time "jamming" with Grandma Carson at the piano and Andi on the guitar. It was only natural that a hint of the blues sometimes crept into Andi's musical creations.

Oddly, musical ability skipped her father's generation. Both he and his sister enjoyed listening to all kinds of music but had no inclination to make their own. Her dad told her that God had saved it up, so she could have a double helping of talent.

She played for much of the afternoon, only occasionally digging through a songbook to read the notes. Although she had taken years of piano lessons and could read music extremely well, Andi played predominately by ear, instinctively playing the notes and cords that she heard in her mind.

She played and sang hymns, some of her own songs, and some of the blues her grandmother had taught her. Then, just randomly playing cords, she hit a combination that triggered a new creation. As her fingers flowed across the keyboard, the melody took form, bursting from her mind to fill the room with music, flooding her heart with joy and thanksgiving.

As the last delicate notes faded away, she felt tears of happiness well up in her eyes. "Thank you, Lord. Thank you from the depths of my soul." In her heart, she seemed to hear a quiet, gentle voice whisper, "You're welcome." Laughing, she spun around on the piano stool, which raised the seat slightly. With a giggle, she spun back the other way.

Calming, she ran through the first few lines of the song again. "Now for the words." In the past, the music had usually come easily; the lyrics had not. She might spend ten minutes to a few days composing the music for a song and weeks trying to come up with the words, often turning in the end to someone else to write them.

Not this time. The words flowed so quickly she could barely keep up. "Wait a minute!" She jumped up and ran to the kitchen cabinet where Dawn stored office supplies. Grabbing a pad and pencil, she sat down on the couch and scribbled the phrases that seemed to flow out of a hidden spring. When she was done, she looked at what she had written. It was a song about Jesus and his wonderful love, the first gospel song she had ever written.

Her hands unsteady, she returned to the piano and put the words together with the music. It took a few times through to get the phrasing and tempo right, but when she finished, she knew it was good.

"Oh, my," she breathed, awed and a little shaken by what had just transpired. "Is this where I'm supposed to go now?" She took a deep breath. "I'll have to think about this, Lord. I know I gave my life to you yesterday, and I want to do what you want me to, but I'm going to need a little time to sort things out."

Her gaze fell on Dawn's stereo, which included a tape player. Recording the song would help her to remember it. She looked through the stereo cabinet, finding some blank tapes but no microphone.

Digging through the junk drawer, she again came up empty handed, but when she checked the garage, she hit pay dirt. On a shelf between a box of magazines from the sixties and a box of old kerosene lamp chimneys, sat a carton labeled "household electronic stuff." Beneath a small roll of speaker wire, two coiled phone cords, and a couple of phone jacks was the microphone and its attached cord.

After recording the song and playing it back, Andi allowed herself a satisfied smile. It wasn't just a good song; it was a very good song. And it didn't sound half bad even recorded on a home system.

Anticipation spiraled through her, a sense of creative excitement she had not experienced in a very long time. She wanted to sit back down at the piano and play for a few more hours but her body demanded a rest. Curling up on the couch, her thoughts drifted back to her childhood, recalling memories that had lain dormant for years.

In her mind's eye, she relived a poignant afternoon spent with her great-grandmother, sitting together on the porch swing of this very house, looking through old family pictures. She had been ten; Granny Mae, ninety-one. Speaking in a whispery voice, the elderly lady shared stories of her youth, reminiscing about her own parents and grandparents, hardy Texas pioneers.

They came across a portrait taken soon after her marriage, and her great-grandmother's eyes filled with a soft, distant light. Her thoughts far away, Granny Mae slowly told her of the man Andi had never known. Gazing beyond the colorful flowers that filled the corners of the yard, she took her back across time to the day they met, when Great-grandpa Buck spent half a month's wages to out-bid five other men for her box supper and the plea-sure of her company at the church social. Through those ancient eyes and cherished memories, Andi met the handsome cowboy, poor but proud and full of dreams, his heart captured the first time he saw the new school teacher.

They had more than their share of hardships. Four children came into the world, and two of them soon passed on into the next. They bought a little place and saw it grow, then times got bad, and they lost it all. But love endured. He went back to being a cowboy, working another man's stock, living on another man's land, earning his way and providing for his family. He never again possessed land of his own, but it didn't matter, for after he was gone, Granny Mae was still given a home on the ranch, a place secured by the sweat of his brow and the faithful-ness of his heart.

Andi would never forget, how, even after twenty years

without her man beside her, Granny Mae's eyes glowed with a love undimmed by time. She confessed that not a day went by that she didn't think of him, miss him, and long to be in his arms again. Less than a month later, she died quietly in her sleep, and her wish came true at last.

Andi swallowed hard, trying to dislodge the lump in her throat. "I want a love like that, Lord," she whispered. "A love that endures no matter what. A love to pass on." Her voice broke as yearning filled her heart. "I want it more than anything in the world."

Eight

❦

Early Friday afternoon, Wade pulled away from the tractor dealer's, the box of parts sitting in the back of the Blazer. "It still amazes me how much a few puny parts can cost. I suppose when the tractor costs fifty to sixty thousand dollars, the parts are bound to be expensive, but it still seems excessive. No wonder so many farmers go under each year."

He glanced in the outside mirror and changed lanes, then gave her an apologetic smile. "Excuse me for griping. Comes with the territory when you're around a farmer or a rancher. If we're not complaining about costs or low prices, we'll bellyache about the weather."

"That's okay," Andi said with a teasing smile. "I have a toy tractor you can borrow, if it will make you feel better. No spare parts needed."

He laughed. "Actually, I have a couple of those myself. How many stuffed animals did you say you got this week?"

"Twenty-three, I think. And all kinds of other stuff, much of it homemade. Everything from a jar of 'Elma's special watermelon pickles' to afghans. There are a handful of sketches and a couple of small oil paintings—nice peaceful country scenes to help me mend. A couple of folks wrote poems and hundreds shared scripture verses to encourage me. I've read cards and letters until my eyes crossed. It always amazes me when people take the time to write, but when they send gifts, especially the homemade ones, it blows me away."

"There's no way you can answer all those letters personally. How do you handle it?"

"To most of them, I'll send autographed pictures with a little printed note thanking them for their letter and telling them that I'm doing much better. I have a secretary in Nashville who takes care of addressing all the envelopes and actually mailing everything. In addition to the photos, I intend to write to the ones who sent gifts. I've typed a basic letter on Dawn's computer and will add something personal to each one. It still takes time, but those folks put in a lot more time on my gift. I'm trying to finish as many each day as I can because I won't be able to do them once I go back to work."

"Any idea when that's going to be?"

"I might know more after I see Doc today. I know I'm not ready yet because my strength isn't where it should be, but I also know I'm improving. Don't worry, I'm not going to rush back before I'm able." She smiled and gave him a wink. "I'm having too much fun."

"Then I'll have to think of more ways to keep you entertained. Why don't you bring Dawn out Sunday afternoon, and we'll have a fish fry. I've got a mess of catfish in the freezer."

"Somehow I don't picture you as a fisherman."

Wade laughed. "I'm not, but I love catfish. So I cheat. I buy them at the catfish farm at the lake. They take care of the catching, cleaning, and deboning. All I have to do is cook 'em and eat 'em. And I don't do half bad if I do say so myself."

"Especially on the eating part." She flashed him a grin.

"Well, I can put quite a few away." He turned into the parking lot of the doctor's office, parked the Blazer, and shut off the ignition. "Do you want me to come in with you?"

She glanced at her watch. "There's no need. We're right on time."

"I don't mind keeping you company while you wait."

"I don't have to wait very long. They've been wonderful about protecting my privacy. I go inside through the back door, and they take me right to a room. That way, I don't have to worry about picking up some new germ or having a lobby full of patients recognize me."

"Pays to be a star, huh?" he said with a smile.

"Sometimes." She put on a giant pair of sunglasses and covered her hair with a plain brown scarf. She looked at him, seeing the question in his eyes. "In case I meet someone in the hall." She opened the door and hopped out. "I'll be back as soon as I can."

The checkup went quickly. Doctor Curtis had helped bring Andi into the world and told her he was pleased she was going to stay in it for a while. He commented right away on her improved color and noted a sparkle in her eyes that hadn't been there before. "It wouldn't have anything to do with that young man who brought you today, would it?"

Andi smiled, enjoying his banter, and teased back. "What were you doing, Doc? Peeking out the back door?" When he nodded, she shrugged lightly. "He's just an old friend from high school."

"Humph." The doctor peered at her over the half-sized reading glasses perched on his nose. "Takes more than a friend to put that kind of glimmer in a woman's eyes."

"I will admit it has been very nice to get reacquainted."

The nurse came in and took some blood, and the doctor examined Andi's lungs. "They still sound clear, and your throat looks fine. Have you been doing any singing?"

"Some. I've been playing the piano quite a bit. Wrote a couple of new songs this week."

"Working on a new album?" he asked as he scribbled some notes in her chart.

"I'm not sure yet, but it's nice to be writing again. I haven't done that in a while."

"Hard to be creative when you're sick. Judging from the information the doctor in Tucson sent me, you had been sick for awhile before you wound up in the hospital. How's your energy level?"

"Getting better almost every day. I've been taking short walks, increasing the distance gradually. I try to rest when I start getting tired instead of waiting until I'm worn out, but sometimes that's hard to do. I like to finish something once I start."

"Andrea, it's very important that you don't allow yourself to become overtired. If you try to rush your recovery, you'll wind up sick again. I know you miss being in the thick of everything, but you were suffering from a major case of exhaustion before you ever became anemic or came down with pneumonia. You have to slow your pace, young lady, or you'll burn out completely," he said sternly. His expression softened. "Perhaps it's time to ease up on your career and find a husband."

Andi laughed. "You never were subtle, Doc."

104

"I plan on retiring in four years, and it would be mighty nice to bring at least one of your babies into the world."

The nurse opened the door and handed him the lab report. He studied it thoughtfully. "Your numbers are improving, but they're not quite where they need to be. Still taking your vitamins?"

"Faithfully. If I forget, Dawn reminds me. She's a vitamin junkie. May I drive now?"

"Yes, you may drive, but no long trips by yourself. Don't take off to El Paso or Dallas. And, I want to see you next week." He stood and patted her on the shoulder. "I expect that in another couple of weeks I can turn you loose, but only if you keep taking care of yourself."

"I will. Scouts honor." She held up two fingers, frowned, and made it three. It had been too many years since she'd been a Brownie Scout to remember the pledge sign.

He walked to the door and looked back at her over his shoulder. "Give my best to Wade. Tell him to stub his toe or something so I can see him. If all my patients were as healthy as he is, I'd go broke." He looked over his reading glasses and winked. "If he's smart, he won't let you get away."

After Doctor Curtis left the room, Andi dressed quickly, tucking her bright red polo shirt into her blue jeans, donned her sunglasses and scarf, and hurried out the back door.

Wade had lowered the back of his bucket seat and was reclining comfortably with his taupe felt hat pulled down over his eyes. She paused a few seconds, admiring the way his light green Western shirt fit his muscular torso. The day was warm, and he had rolled up his sleeves to the middle of his forearms. When she opened her door, he pushed his hat back and sat up, raising the seat back upright. "Hi, darlin'. How did it go?"

The warmth and tenderness in his eyes and smile made Andi's heart do a funny little flip. She suddenly imagined him holding a tiny baby in his arms, their baby. Her heart began to tap dance. *Blast you, Doc, for putting ideas into my head.* "It went fine. Blood count is up. He said I could start driving, so looks like you're gonna lose your wheels."

"Fine by me. I'm glad you're improving." He glanced at his watch. "We've got about three hours until dinner. What do you want to do?"

"Go to the mall. I need to buy a couple of dresses for church."

"I don't know if I like the glint in your eye, woman. Something tells me you're going to find more than a couple of dresses." He started the Blazer and backed out of the parking space.

Andi laughed and pulled off her scarf. They chatted about the doctor and the way Sidell had grown until they reached the mall.

He parked in front of the main department store and warily eyed the building.

"You don't like shopping, do you?"

"I don't mind if it doesn't take long to find what I need."

"Typical man. You go in, get something the right size and color, buy it, and leave. But a woman shops differently, right?"

"Right. At least Aunt Della does. Takes her forever."

"Oh, you poor thing." She leaned across the console between their seats and tickled his chin. "Be forewarned. I have a very large clothing budget."

He looked down at her, his expression resigned. "So what

you're telling me is that we're going to be here 'til supper time. You realize you're going to have to pay me to carry all those packages. And don't forget my patience. That has to be added in."

"A kiss when we're done."

He gave her a you've-got-to-be-kidding look and shook his head. "It's going to take more Yankee dimes than that."

Hearing the old Southern term for a kiss made her smile. "Two?"

"Nope."

She looked at her watch. "One for every hour that we're here."

He considered her offer. "Not enough. I'm the bodyguard, too, remember?"

"I usually pay my bodyguard in real money."

"I hope so. What about the guy who carries the packages?"

"One and the same. So you shouldn't get more because you're doing two jobs."

"Call it inflation. One Yankee dime for every half hour."

"It's a deal."

He removed his hat and fastened it in the hat rack in the ceiling above the console, brim up, the crown sitting through the loop of metal that held it in place. Glancing in the mirror, he fluffed his hair with his fingers where it had been smashed by the hat.

"Quit primping," ordered Andi with a grin. "Come on, slave. Time's a wastin'."

❧

Wade decided that watching Andi shop was like watching a tornado rip through town. She flew around the clothes racks, picking up anything that caught her eye, then headed for the dressing room, barely able to see over the stack in her arms, with him trailing along behind. At first, he hovered nearby, feeling self-conscious under the sometimes appreciative, sometimes questioning glances of women shoppers and the sales clerks. Then Andi popped out of the dressing room to get his opinion on a dress.

He figured she knew it looked great, but he appreciated her including him in the process. After she went back into the dressing room, he looked around and realized that by making a point of showing him the dress, she had validated his reason for being there in the other women's eyes. She bought the dress and several other items, then it was on to the next store and the same routine.

She pulled one dress off the rack, a pretty blue print with short sleeves, a shirt-style collar and a slightly gathered skirt. Just right for church, he thought, and figured she would get it. She took one look at the price and put it back. "What's wrong?"

"It's a designer label and costs four hundred dollars. Even I have my limits, and I don't want anyone thinking I'm trying to show off."

She disappeared into the dressing room, and he sat down in a chair conveniently placed a short distance from the main dressing room door. Setting the two large plastic shopping bags on the floor beside him, he relaxed, stretching his long legs out in front of him.

He hoped she would come out as she had done in the last store. There was a little black silk number he was interested in seeing, along with some other fancy ones. He supposed she might wear them on stage or somewhere in Nashville. Just thinking about her going back to work made him feel as if he had stepped on thin ice and fallen into a freezing river.

She walked out of the dressing room wearing a yellow dress with a wide ruffle at the neck and one at the bottom of each long sleeve. Wide horizontal ruffles covered the skirt from the dropped waist almost to her ankles. She stopped in front of the three-way mirror, turning from side to side. "What do you think?" she asked with a frown.

He tried valiantly to keep a straight face. "You want an honest opinion?" When she nodded, Wade took a deep breath. "Well, if you add a few feathers to your hair, you could be in the Fourth of July parade."

She lifted her brow. "As?"

"A baby chick. Or you could cut the bill off an old cap, dye it yellow, and tie it around your face and go as a duck." He chuckled as she glared at him and looked in the mirror again.

She wiggled, sending the ruffles flapping, and grinned. "A bit much, isn't it."

He nodded, laughing out loud as she waddled into the dressing room. A few minutes later, she was back, wearing a beautiful magenta dress with a gauzy print overskirt. "Now, that's nice. Feminine. And it's a pretty color on you. I like it." He was surprised to see how his praise made her face light up. Surely she heard compliments all the time.

She went back to try on something else, and he made faces at a toddler sitting in a stroller in the next aisle. He and the little fellow were busy entertaining each other when she returned. Wade glanced up and did a double take. Sucking in a deep breath, he sat up straight and stared.

The yellow dress had been a bit too much, but the black silk one was...a bit. Period. Although the neckline was wide, revealing most of her shoulders, it wasn't low. And though the material skimmed her figure, it wasn't too tight but merely flattering—as far as it went. He'd seen blouses that were longer.

"Do you like it?" she asked, uncertainty in her voice.

"Oh, baby, do I ever." He picked up the bags, walked over, and stood behind her, attempting to shield her from the view of others in the store. "But I don't want another man to see you in that dress." He knew he sounded possessive and was revealing more of his feelings than he should, but he couldn't help it. He watched her face in the mirror as delicate color spread over her cheeks.

"I'm sorry. I'm not trying to embarrass you."

"It's all right. A few weeks ago, I wouldn't have thought twice about buying this to wear in the show. Now, I'm uncomfortable in it. I was before you said anything."

"You're beautiful in it, Andi, but other men won't be able to see past the outside to the godly woman inside."

"I guess I have a lot more than just dusty corners for God to clean out. I have a lot to learn—or maybe learn over," she said sadly. "And a few real closets to go through."

"Hey, wisdom comes over a lifetime. That's why we've got the Holy Spirit to guide us. We always have something new to learn or overcome." He leaned over so his mouth was close to her ear, his voice dropping low and ragged, "Now, go get out of that thing before I revert to a cave man."

CHAPTER

Nine

❦

They hit another store, where she found some Sunday dresses she was happy with, and he fussed at her for trying to do too much. "It's habit. I usually only have an hour or two to spend before I have to get back and do a show or meet some other commitment."

By the time they stopped for cookies and something to drink, they were both loaded down with bags and boxes. He also thought she was beginning to look tired. "Had enough?"

"Almost. I want to look at that denim vest over there in the window. I love all the embroidery on it."

He smiled indulgently. "About the time I think I've figured out your style, you find something totally different."

"I'm eclectic. What I wear depends on my mood. I might feel free as the wind—

"The magenta dress."

She nodded. "Or like a rock, firmly fixed."

"The gray dress for church."

"Not bad for a cowboy."

He glanced around, noting that more and more people were staring in their direction. "Uh-oh. Looks like you've been recognized."

"Yep. It's show time." Andi smiled at a girl in her late teens a few tables over. Encouraged by her friends, the young woman finally worked up the nerve to come over.

"Excuse me, miss, but are you Andi Carson, the singer?" she asked, sounding polite and poised.

"Yes, I am."

"Oh my gosh!" The girl turned toward her friends and squealed, jumping up and down. "It is her!" she screamed. "It's Andi Carson!" She turned back to Andi. "Oh, Miss Carson, I love your music. I have everything you've ever done. Can I have your autograph?"

"Sure." Andi dug a pen out of her purse. "Do you have anything for me to write on?"

The girl grabbed a napkin out of the hand of a middle-aged man at the table next to them. He stared for a second, then started laughing. "Will this work?"

"It'll do. Just don't forget and wipe mustard on it," she teased.

"Oh, I won't. I'll keep it always."

Andi cocked her head and studied the girl for a minute. It was hard to tell her age. She had long blond hair, green eyes, and was pretty even with minimal makeup. She had a lilting, musical voice, but there was something else about it—something Andi couldn't quite pinpoint—that intrigued her. Somehow, she knew the girl was a singer. She didn't have the vaguest idea of how she knew it, but she did.

"I'm so glad you're feeling better, Miss Carson. We were so worried about you." By now the girl's friends and at least twenty other people had congregated around the table.

"Thanks. I was worried there for a while, too. What's your name?"

"Nicki Alexander."

Andi signed the napkin and handed it to her, asking casually, "Do you sing, Nicki?"

"A...a little." She turned pale and began to tremble.

"She's really good, Miss Carson," one of her friends chimed in. "She won the talent shows all through junior high and high school and always got the lead in our school musicals. Now she sings solos a lot at church."

"Do you play an instrument, Nicki?"

"Y-yes, ma'am. Piano and guitar. I played saxophone in the school band."

"Have you graduated?"

The girl nodded.

"How old are you?"

"Nineteen." Her voice quivered, and she clenched her hands, unknowingly crumpling the napkin with Andi's autograph.

"Take voice lessons?"

She shook her head. "We couldn't afford voice and piano, too. There are five other kids in the family."

Andi took Nicki's ice-cold hand and looked into her eyes. It was there, the intense desire, the need to free the music burning in her soul. "Do you want to be a musician, Nicki?" she asked quietly.

Tears welled up in the girl's eyes. "More than anything in the world," she whispered. She cleared her throat and blinked hard. "It's like I have to make music, Miss Carson. It's in my head all the time. Sometimes the songs have words and sometimes they don't, but they just seem to pour out."

Andi squeezed her hand and released it. "I know exactly what you mean. Tell you what; ask this handsome cowboy here to tear off part of that sack and write your name and phone number on it and tuck it in his pocket so we won't loose it." She glanced around and smiled at the crowd, then looked back at Nicki. "I'd like to sit down and talk to you where it's a little quieter. Would there be a good time this weekend to call you?"

"Anytime. I won't set foot out of the house. You call when it's convenient for you."

Good girl. You think fast on your feet. "I'll try not to make you wait too long." Andi glanced at Wade, who had already torn off a big piece of the sack.

"Do you have another pen?" he asked, his eyes full of admiration and affection.

"Always," she said with a laugh, digging in her purse. She tossed it to him, smiling her appreciation, then turned to the next person, immediately giving him her full attention.

Wade watched as Nicki started to write her name. The poor kid was shaking so hard, Andi probably wouldn't be able to read it. "Here, why don't I do that. It's hard to write while standing up." He jotted down her name and phone number, folded the paper precisely and tucked it into his shirt pocket, fastening the pearl snap on the flap. "There," he said, patting his pocket, rustling the paper. "Safe and secure. I promise I won't let it go through the washing machine."

Nicki managed a feeble smile, then she leaned closer and whispered, "Will she really call?"

"She'll call." He had never been more certain of anything. "I can't promise it will be today, though. She's not completely recovered and has to stop whenever she starts getting tired." He glanced at Andi. "Which looks like it's going to be soon, but I reckon she'll push it this time. Now, go over there and calm down before you try to drive home."

"My friend is driving," she said, straightening, looking dazed.

Wade laughed softly. "That's good." He hoped the friend she meant wasn't the one who was dancing around, hugging Andi's autograph to her heart. He decided Nicki needed something to do. "Could I ask a favor?"

She took a deep breath and shook her head, as if to clear it. Her eyes widened as she seemed to focus on Wade's face for the first time. A tinge of pink touched her cheeks. "Uh, sure."

"See the embroidered denim vest over in that window? Would you run over there and ask how much it is and see if they have a size eight?"

She glanced at Andi and grinned. "I'll be right back."

"Thanks." He watched her blond ponytail bounce as she hurried over to the store, then turned his attention back to Andi. She smiled and chatted with each person for a minute as she signed an autograph for them on anything at hand—napkins, sales receipts, sacks, even the back of one kid's T-shirt. He scanned the crowd, which seemed to keep growing. Her fans ranged in age from eight to eighty, and practically everyone had a kind word for her. The few who didn't seemed merely awe-struck.

Nicki slipped up beside him. "The vest is on sale for forty-five dollars, and they have a size eight."

"Thank you. Could I ask you to go get it for me? I don't want to leave Andi alone." When she nodded, her eyes shining with pleasure, he dug out his wallet and handed her more than enough to cover the price and tax. "Do they gift wrap?"

"I'm not sure, but they do have gold gift boxes. I saw some on the shelf behind the counter."

He glanced at Andi to make certain she wasn't listening. "If they gift wrap, pick out some pretty paper, maybe flowers or something. If they don't, the gift box will do, but ask them to put it in a sack when they're done."

"Gotcha." As she hurried off, her friends joined her. She glanced back at Wade, grinned, and started talking a-mile-a-minute, obviously filling them in on what she was doing.

It took a while for Nicki and her entourage to return. By then Wade had grown concerned about the number of people lined up for autographs. Practically everyone who walked by either recognized her, or stopped and asked someone else about her and ultimately got in the line.

He noted fatigue creeping into Andi's smile. There was no way she could keep this up long enough to take care of them all. He leaned over before she looked up at the next person. "You're going to have to stop in a minute."

"I'm all right. I don't want to turn anyone away."

"You'll have to. There are at least fifty people in line, and it keeps growing. Five more, and that's it."

She took a deep breath, and he noticed her hand shake minutely when she lifted it. "Ten more. And I promise I'll quit."

He didn't like it, but he knew the stubborn tilt of her chin meant there could be no arguing with her. "Ten, it is. But not one person more."

He stood up, counting down the line, and made a mental notation of who would be the last lucky person today. Gathering up the boxes and sacks with all of their purchases, he walked over to the nearby table where Nicki and her friends sat. "She's getting tired. I'm going to take her out of here in a few minutes."

"That may not be easy." Nicki glanced at the line. "We know those guys about half-way down. They graduated three years ago. They can get downright nasty when they want to."

Wade followed her gaze to the three men. He had already singled them out as troublemakers. One was slight, but the other two were big, strong farm boys. Judging from the way they laughed and poked each other in the ribs, they were thinking up any number of suggestive things to say to Andi.

"I saw them," he said gravely. "You girls want to help me get her out of here?"

"We can carry all your stuff. Then your hands will be free in case you need to punch them out," said one of Nicki's friends, a gleam of anticipation in her eyes.

"I don't expect it will come to that, but it would be a big help if you took care of these. Then all I'll have to worry about will be Andi." He looked way down the mall toward the entrance where they came in and sighed. Some bodyguard he was. They had over half the length of the mall to cover before they reached the Blazer.

He dug his keys out of his pocket and handed them to Nicki. "I've got a dark blue Chevy Blazer in the third space, second row, outside that far door." He gave her the license number and showed her which keys to use in the door and the ignition. "Bring it around to the side opposite the theater, and we'll come out that exit."

The four girls grabbed their purses and all of Wade's packages and rushed off down the mall. To his surprise, none of them giggled or made light of the situation. Their expressions were determined, almost grim. He figured he didn't have to worry about them taking anything, not with Nicki's telephone number—and her dreams—in his breast pocket.

He walked over to the people in line, starting behind the person they had decided would be last, explaining the situation. "I'm sorry, folks, but Miss Carson is going to have to call it a day. She's still recovering and has been warned by her doctor to take it easy. Can't get too tired or she'll have a relapse. Maybe she can set up something in a few weeks, and you can come back and talk to her then."

Most of the people were disappointed, but understood. As those near the front of the line started to disperse, the ones in the back figured out what was going on and began to drift away, too. All except the three cowboys he had expected to cause a problem.

"Hey, you can't do that. We've been waiting ten minutes," protested the smaller of the three men. "We're not leavin' until we get to talk to her, are we, boys? We'll just go pay her a little visit right now." He poked the biggest man in the back, and he started to move forward.

Wade stepped into his path. "Miss Carson is tired. She won't be doing any more visiting with her fans today." He stood eye to eye with the younger man, who probably outweighed him by about twenty pounds. It didn't matter.

"I don't give a hang about anybody else, but she's going to talk to us."

"No, she's not." Wade stood his ground, his voice firm, his expression implacable. Out of the corner of his eye, he saw the other large man take a couple of steps backward, his hands raised slightly, fingers open and palms turned forward in a gesture indicating he didn't want any part of a fight.

The man in front of Wade sneered. "You think you can stop all three of us?"

"I know I can." *I'm protecting the woman I love.* Adrenaline surged through him, but he remained still. He didn't want to fight, but he would if he had to. He had been in more brawls in his younger days than he liked to admit. He knew how to hold his own.

I Ie saw uncertainty creep into the man's eyes. "It's Friday night," Wade said softly. "You don't want to go partying with a busted nose, do you?" The man shifted his stance, relaxing slightly, and for a second, Wade thought he was going to walk away.

"Billy Bob, don't let this jerk buffalo you." The smaller man glared at his companion. "Hit him."

Billy Bob stiffened, flexing his fingers.

"You always take orders from him?" Wade asked casually, preparing to ward off a blow.

"I don't take orders from nobody."

"Then why don't you act more intelligently than your friend here and leave Miss Carson alone? You aren't going to make a good impression with the lady by starting a fight and embarrassing her. You'll make more points by being considerate of her health and her feelings."

"We had tickets to her concert in Fort Worth," Billy Bob complained.

"It will probably be rescheduled when she is completely well. Upsetting her will only delay her recovery." Wade shifted slightly, so the man had a clear view of Andi. "Does she look tired to you?"

"Yeah, she's kinda droopin'." He scratched the back of his head.

"Billy Bob!" the short man whined.

"Shut up, Jinx." Billy Bob spun around and grabbed his friend by the shoulder, shoving him into motion. "Let's go. I ain't being disrespectful to the lady 'cause you got your nose out of joint."

Wade watched them move away down the mall before turning back toward Andi. She was standing by the table observing the confrontation. Several people, both men and women, stood protectively around her, but they moved aside as he hurried toward her. "Thanks, folks. Come on, honey, let's get out of here before that little banty rooster talks those big dumb clucks into doing something else stupid." He heard a few chuckles and caught a few speculative glances as he put his arm around her and propelled her toward the side exit.

"I thought the Blazer was at the other end." She peeked back over her shoulder. "And where is our stuff?"

"Nicki and her friends took care of it. She's bringing the Blazer around here." He looked down at her, relief pouring through him. "I was afraid we might have trouble."

"Are they behind us?"

Wade glanced back. "No."

"Then slow down. My legs aren't as long as yours." She slid her arm around his waist as he eased the pace. "Have I told you lately that you're wonderful?"

He looked down at her and almost tripped over his own feet.

Her face glowed, and pure, undisguised adoration shone in her eyes. His chest swelled with such pride that he was surprised he didn't pop open the snaps on his shirt. "Not that I recall."

"Well, you are. You're the best looking, most wonderful man on earth."

He grinned and tugged on an imaginary hat. "Now you've done it. I can feel my hat gettin' tight already."

"I'll buy you another one."

He pushed open the outside door to find Nicki and her friends huddled beside the Blazer, which she had parked right by the curb in a No Parking area. He was relieved that no one from mall security was in sight.

"Did you have to fight them?"

"No. They protested a little, but decided to be nice."

"Only because Wade convinced them to." Andi winked at the girls. "You missed quite a show. This guy was really something. Thank you, too. Our get-away might not have gone as smoothly without your help."

"Anytime," said one of the girls. "Although I am sorry we missed the man in action." She shot Wade a flirtatious grin.

He felt Andi's fingers dig into his side. *She's jealous,* he thought in amazement. "Aw, it weren't nuthin'," he said playfully. He smiled at the girl, careful not to flirt back, and opened the Blazer door for Andi, assisting her inside. He shut the door and turned to the girls, his expression serious. "I appreciate your help. We're going out to dinner, now, but I expect she'll call you later tonight, Nicki, and set up a time to get together."

"Is she staying here in town?"

"Let's just say she is staying with another friend and let it go at that." He pulled out all the stops and gave them a smile that had proven in the past to completely distract women from whatever they had on their minds. If their dewy-eyed expressions were any indication, it worked.

Ten

❧

A ndi was surprised when Wade pulled up in front of a small Italian restaurant. "I had you pegged as a steak and potatoes man."

"I am, but we eat a lot of that at home, so I usually get something else when I go out. Is this all right? Dawn said you like Italian food."

"About the only kind of food I don't like is anything with curry in it. And I love Italian food."

He flashed her a smile and hopped out of the Blazer, going around the front to open her door. "I haven't been here, but I'm told the food is good. You don't have to dress up, and it's small enough that we won't be mobbed."

"Sounds perfect."

It was. Although the hostess recognized Andi when they stepped through the door, the young woman didn't make a fuss. She simply showed them to a booth in the corner, away from both the kitchen and the other diners, and told her how happy she was to see her feeling better. A few minutes later, the owner, a large man with black hair, a handlebar mustache, and an accent that was a hybrid of Italian and Texas twang, came to thank them for choosing his restaurant and to personally take their order.

"I'll have to take you out more often." Wade plucked a bread stick from the basket in the middle of the table before leaning back against the well-padded vinyl seat. "Basking in your shadow has its benefits."

"Some men would feel threatened."

"Because you're rolling in dough? Or because half the country thinks the sun rises and sets when you tell it to?" he teased.

"Only half?"

"Well, maybe two-thirds. After all, Texas counts for half." He leaned across the table and laid his hand over hers. "Andi, I'm proud of your success and glad people adore you—the well behaved ones anyway." He leaned back again, grabbing another bread stick on the way. "Besides, I know you don't have any control over the sun." The sunshine in his heart was a different story, but he didn't plan on mentioning that.

"And I thought I had you fooled."

They told each other funny stories and laughed and enjoyed the crisp green salad and lasagna, with no worries about time or people or responsibilities. The waitress was attentive but not obtrusive, the lighting was low and romantic, and the muffled voices of the other diners provided a pleasant, relaxed atmosphere. They ate in peace and left in peace.

Wade glanced at her as he drove back through town. She was staring out the window, her expression thoughtful but with a hint of excitement. "You thinking about Nicki?"

She looked at him and smiled. "Yes. I should give her a call before we leave town. It was so strange when I met her today.

Somehow I knew she could sing. She had a quality to her voice that suggested it, but there was something more. I can't quite put my finger on it."

"Sounds like the Lord." He smiled gently at her startled expression. "He's good at revealing things he wants us to know."

She met his gaze briefly before leaning her head back against the seat and staring up at the starry sky. "I think you're right," she murmured, shaking her head in awe. "Now I understand what Dawn was talking about. When I first got here, she was telling me how she knows when the Lord wants her to say something or do something for someone. She said often it's a feeling, but sometimes it's even clearer, like whispers in her heart."

She turned toward him, shifting as much as the seat belt would allow, oblivious to the buckle digging into her hip. "I didn't hear words exactly, but I knew she could sing as surely as if I had heard her. And I felt a strong urge not only to ask her about it, but to do something." She frowned. "But I'm not sure what."

"Listening to her and giving her encouragement is where you have to start. If God wants you to do more, he'll let you know."

Excitement raced through her. "Would you mind going over to see her now?"

"Aren't you tired? You can't push yourself too hard."

"I'm not." She glanced at the clock on the dash. It was only 7:30. "It's early. Besides, I won't ever get to sleep tonight if I don't follow up on this." She remembered how she had been after Kyle had first talked to her. "And poor Nicki will be a basket case. Probably worthless by tomorrow."

"If you agree to leave when I say. I intend to keep your recovery on track whether you do or not."

125

"Trying to get rid of me, Jamison?" she asked with a laugh as he stopped at a red light. The laughter died in her throat when he looked at her.

For a heartbeat, deep, dark pain filled his countenance. Then he smiled, but the warmth did not reach his eyes, did not take away the sorrow lingering there. "Naw, I'll let you hang around as long as you want."

Even for a lifetime? Yearning flooded her heart, an ocean of need that made her desire to sing seem like a puddle. *I love you.* Her heart demanded she voice the words, but her head vetoed the idea. Perhaps she was only imagining the depth of his feelings, seeing what she wanted to see. *Give him time. Don't scare him off.* She didn't know if it was the Lord holding her back or her own fear. She glanced out the window, taking a minute to gather her composure.

"Well, that's good, 'cause I'm not in any hurry to leave." She tried to make her voice sound light and playful. His sharp glance told her she had almost succeeded. "I'm beginning to enjoy the slower-paced life."

"It will wear off." Wade unsnapped his shirt pocket and withdrew the paper with Nicki's phone number. Handing it to her, he pointed to the cellular phone. "Help yourself."

She picked up the phone and punched in the numbers. When Nicki answered on the first ring, Andi smiled at Wade and told the girl what they had in mind. Nicki promptly invited them over, giving her directions. They arrived at the house less than ten minutes later. It was a modest home, but in good condition.

When Nicki showed them inside, her father and mother were waiting. Mr. Alexander approached Andi cautiously, carefully inspecting her features. She waited a minute, then gave him a big smile. "Hello, Mr. Alexander. I'm Andi Carson."

His solemn face broke into an astonished smile. "Mama, it is her! Look at those dimples." He shook his head. "I'm sorry, ma'am, but when Nicki told us about meeting you and said you were coming over, we were scared somebody was trying to play a cruel joke."

"You're wise to be cautious, sir." She pulled out her wallet and flipped it open to reveal her driver's license. "This might help."

Wade peeked over her shoulder. "Wouldn't you know it? Even her driver's license picture looks good." He held out his hand to Nicki's father. "Wade Jamison. I'm a friend of Andi's."

"You a musician, too?" the older man asked as he shook Wade's hand.

"Strictly amateur. I'm a rancher. Have a place south of Buckley."

"Please sit down." Mrs. Alexander motioned toward a brown love seat placed at a right angle to the matching sofa. "Can I get you some coffee or anything?"

"No thanks. We just finished dinner." Andi glanced across the room and laughed. Five faces of various ages peeked around the edge of a doorway. From her angle, it looked as if they were stacked one on top of the other. "This must be the rest of the family."

"Y'all come on in," said Nicki. "But behave."

The other children trooped in. They appeared to range in age from six to sixteen. "Did you really come to our house to hear Nicki sing?" asked the youngest, a little boy.

"Yes, I did."

"How come?"

Andi glanced at Wade. He didn't say anything, but she saw encouragement in his eyes. She took a deep breath to allay a flutter of nervousness. She had promised the Lord she wouldn't hide her faith and her love for him, but this was the first time in many years that she had let her light shine before strangers.

"Because I think God wants me to," she said, looking at the youngster.

"Oh." The little boy tipped his head to one side. "Did you read that in the Bible somewhere? Does it say you're supposed to go listen to people sing?"

Andi looked quickly at Nicki and her parents. They appeared mildly amused at the question but also curious as to what Andi was going to say. At least they didn't seem upset. "No, it was just a feeling I got today when I talked to your sister."

"Oh." The child seemed to accept the answer without question. "Is she gonna be a star like you?"

"I don't know. We'll just have to wait and see."

"Grownups say that a lot."

She laughed softly. "Yes, I suppose we do."

"Okay, kids, you've met Miss Carson. Now run on back to the rec room and watch your video." Mr. Alexander's voice was quiet but firm. "We don't want to waste her time." As the children reluctantly left the room, he had a kind word or smile for each of them. He looked back at Andi. "Will my wife and I be in the way?"

"No, by all means, please stay. I'm sure Nicki will be more comfortable with you here." Andi looked at Nicki and smiled warmly, trying to ease the girl's tension. "I know you're nervous, but try to relax. This is not a make-it-or-lose-it moment. If things don't come together right now, we'll try another time.

How long have you taken piano?"

"Six years. I didn't start until I was twelve. That's when we got ours. But I'd been picking out songs on my grandma's piano for a long time before that."

"You play by ear?"

"Yes, ma'am. But my teacher always made me sight-read the music before she would play it for me." A smile flickered across Nicki's face.

"Smart lady. I coasted through two years of music lessons before my teacher figured out I could barely read a note. She had a habit of playing each piece first, so I could hear how it was supposed to sound." Andi smiled ruefully. "After I heard it, I didn't need to read the music. Which do you like best, the guitar or piano?"

"I like them both. I guess it depends on my mood and the song."

"Are you more relaxed with one of them?"

"Yes, the guitar."

"Then let's start with it."

Nicki walked over beside the piano, picked up one of the two guitars leaning against the wall, and returned to the chair across from Andi and Wade.

"Play anything you like, something you're comfortable with and that will help you warm up. I'm in no hurry, so take your time. Sing whenever you feel like it."

Nicki placed her fingers on the strings, strumming a few chords and adjusting the tuning slightly. Once she was satisfied with the pitch, she began to play. She missed a few notes at first, but soon she was lost in the music. The tempo was moderate, the melody intricate yet soothing. The song made Andi think of the **creek** where she and Wade had taken a walk. Bubbling, happy, yet peaceful. When Nicki lifted her fingers after the last chord, she paused, then slowly raised her gaze.

"Very nice. Is that one of yours?" asked Andi. When Nicki nodded, she continued, "I don't think I ever asked what type of music you like to sing."

"Mostly country and gospel. I guess I'm kinda like you. I like a variety." Relaxing more, she flashed Andi a real smile and began playing a lively tune.

Andi recognized it immediately as one of the first songs she had recorded.

Nicki pursed her lips, frowning mildly. "Without the backup guitar, it doesn't sound quite right."

"Well, that's easy to remedy." Wade hopped up from the couch and walked over to the piano to get the other guitar. He grinned at Andi when he dropped down beside her again. "Didn't know I could play your songs, did you?"

She shook her head, watching in fascination as he nodded to Nicki. The girl started again, and he joined in with the second part, playing each note and chord perfectly. Nicki grinned and so did Wade. Laughing, Andi held up her hands. "All right, all right. I'm impressed with both of you. Can you sing that one?"

"I can't do it as good as you can."

"Everybody has their own style. Hit it, kid. Show me your stuff."

"Okay." Nicki took a deep breath and played the intro. Wade joined in as she belted out the bouncy song about a girl's futile efforts to capture the attention of the boy next door. She had perfect pitch, and her voice was strong with a hint of vibrato.

After the first line or two, she relaxed, giving the song a sassy nuance all her own.

A conflicting mix of emotions rushed through Andi—thrill at discovering a wonderfully talented performer, satisfaction and excitement because she would be able to make Nicki's way easier than hers had been, and a twinge of rivalry. This girl was going to give them all strong competition.

The song ended, and Wade looked at Andi, grinning from ear to ear. "Is the lady good or what?"

Jealousy pricked her, but it had nothing to do with Nicki's singing. She forced herself to ignore it, confident God wouldn't have led her to Nicki if it meant losing Wade. "She's better than good. She's fantastic. And I'm glad I recorded that song before you had a chance at it, young lady."

Nicki gasped and clamped her hand over her mouth. A tear slid down her cheek, followed quickly by several more as she looked at her parents. They were of no help. They sat rooted to the sofa, completely dumbfounded. Andi gave them a few minutes to get their bearings.

"Uh…" Mr. Alexander stopped and cleared his throat. "I don't mean any offense, ma'am, but I don't want my girl working in any honky-tonks."

"She shouldn't have to, not if we handle things right. I'm staying with my cousin in Buckley. Nicki, I'd like you to come over so we can record a tape. It won't be anything fancy, not like something produced in a studio, but it will give my manager an idea of how great you are. Once Kyle hears you, he'll probably have you on the next plane to Nashville.

"You don't have to sign with Kyle, but I can vouch for him. His entertainment company is one of the best in the business.

He handles recording contracts, concert bookings, publicity, and promotion, all the business stuff. He's very good at his job, and perhaps even more important, he listens to me. If I ask him not to book you in bars or honky-tonks, he won't. You will definitely need a manager. It's hard to get anywhere in this business without one, but if you find for some reason you don't like him, there are others I can recommend.

"Kyle runs the business end of things, but I have the final say on what goes into the performances, including the opening acts. When I got sick, we released everyone who had signed onto the tour with us so they could find other work. We will be trying to reschedule as many of the canceled performances as possible after I'm able to go back to work, and we will need someone to open the show."

"And you want me to do some of them?" Nicki whispered.

"I can't promise yet, but I'd like to see what we can pull together. It will take a lot of hard work, mostly from you and your manager. My biggest contribution will probably be opening the door."

"How can I ever thank you, Miss Carson?"

"Well, you can start by calling me, Andi. Miss Carson makes me want to look around for my old-maid aunt. Do you work?"

"Yes. Three days a week at the bank. I'm off on Mondays and Fridays."

"Could you come over Monday morning?"

"Sure. What time?"

"Let's make it nine. In the meantime, think about what songs you want to sing. You can use some that other people have done, but you should have some of your own, too. A variety is good, so you can show your vocal range as well as style changes." She took a small notepad from her purse and wrote down Dawn's phone number, address, and the directions to get there. "I'm sure you realize we need to keep the address and phone number confidential. Please don't even tell your friends where I'm staying. I appreciate my fans, but as you saw today, I wouldn't be able to get any rest if my location is public knowledge. And right now, I have to be able to rest whenever I need it."

"Don't worry. We won't tell."

Andi looked at Nicki's parents. "You're welcome to come over, too, if you want."

"Thank you, but I expect we'll let Nicki handle this on her own," said Mrs. Alexander, dabbing her eyes with a wadded up Kleenex. "It's hard to let go, but she's all grown up and needs to make her own decisions."

"I still want your advice." Nicki beamed a smile at her folks. "You know that." She collapsed against the back of the chair. "I can't believe it. I can't believe you're sitting here in our living room, much less offering to be my mentor and a chance to go to Nashville. You don't know how much this means to me."

Andi smiled gently. "Actually, I have a good idea. Once you get started in this business, you'll understand what I mean. I went to Nashville when I was eighteen, right out of high school. I didn't know a single person in Tennessee or in the music industry. It's been a long, hard road, filled with disappointments and sometimes danger, as well as happiness and success. It will give me a great deal of satisfaction to make that way easier for you."

"Do you do this often, Andi?" asked Mr. Alexander.

"I've helped a couple of guitar pickers find good jobs, but that was merely by putting in a word here and there after I heard them play. I've never had the opportunity to work with a new singer like this. It's exciting."

"Not nearly as exciting as it is for us."

Andi laughed and stood. "I'm sure it isn't. We'd better go and let you share the fun with the rest of the family. I know Nicki is dying to call all her friends."

Nicki and her parents walked Andi and Wade to the door. "We won't go outside, so you can leave quietly," said Nicki. "Our next-door neighbor is a big fan of yours, and he has a whole house full of company. He will probably kill me when he finds out you were here."

"Maybe I can meet him another time." Andi stifled a yawn. "When I'm perkier."

They said goodbye, and Wade cupped her elbow as they walked down the steps. Once they were inside the Blazer, he leaned over and whispered, "You're one special lady, Andrea Carson." He kissed her tenderly, almost reverently, touching only her lips with his.

Andi could have sworn the ground shifted. When he ended the kiss and looked down at her, she knew she wore the same dazed expression as he did. "I can see the headlines, now," she said, not even trying to hide her breathlessness. A frown touched his brow, and she smoothed it gently with her fingers. "Country singer dies of heart palpitations after earth-shaking kiss."

He smiled and leaned back in his seat. "That's a pretty long headline."

"They'd probably delete the earth-shaking part."

His smile widened, and he started the Blazer. "Not if they were factual."

She watched him as he backed the Blazer out of the drive. Such a simple thing, observing someone you loved, yet so pleasant.

She didn't think she would ever grow tired of watching the way he moved—strong, confident, precise. She would never become weary of looking at his face, learning each expression—one second, alert and cautious as he pulled out into the street, the next sending her a teasing smile.

"By the way, don't plan on counting that as partial payment for all the work I did today."

"Seems to me that was the equivalent of a whole stack of Yankee dimes."

Turning down the street leading to the freeway, he considered her statement. "Could be. But I figure it was a bonus for sharing you this evening."

She shrugged. "That sounds reasonable."

He looked surprised. "What? Not even a little protest about increased costs?"

She leaned toward him as far as the seat belt and shoulder harness would allow. "Sugar, my mama didn't raise no fool."

When they got back to Dawn's, Wade reached behind the seat and pulled his present out of the paper bag. Smiling, he handed her the gold foil gift box, trimmed with lacy gold ribbon and a bow. "You forgot something at the mall."

"What?" she asked, her expression puzzled.

"Open it and see."

With an excited smile, she eased the ribbon from around the box and set it and the bow carefully aside, then pulled off the lid and folded back the white tissue paper, revealing the embroidered denim vest. "Oh, Wade," she said softly, "it's beautiful."

She lifted it out of the box, holding it closer to the windshield to see better in the street light. "It's even prettier than I thought it would be. You're so sweet." She leaned over the console and kissed him. "Thank you."

"You're welcome. Think it will fit?"

"It should." She scooted forward in the seat and slipped it on. "Perfect."

He glanced at the vest, which did fit well and looked very nice, but he was more interested in the warm glow in her lovely eyes. He cradled her face in his hand. "Perfect," he whispered, before collecting a portion of his day's wages.

Eleven

W hen Wade pulled into the Community Church parking lot Sunday morning, Andi surveyed the building and the people as they greeted each other with smiles. She had spent a great deal of time during her junior high and high school years inside those walls, talking, laughing, and sometimes crying with many of the same people.

The church had a different minister, a man in his mid-thirties. Both Dawn and Wade thought highly of him. Although Andi would have enjoyed seeing their old pastor, she decided it was good he was no longer there. He knew her too well. He would have looked into her eyes and seen the things she had seen, the roads she had traveled.

By the time Wade parked and turned off the engine, the butterflies in her stomach had stirred into a panic. "Are you sure they'll let me through the door?"

He smiled in understanding. "Relax, they'll be thrilled to see you."

"I don't know about that. I suspect some of them think I'm some kind of brazen hussy."

Dawn leaned forward from the back seat and squeezed Andi's shoulder. "If they do, they will keep it to themselves. One of Pastor Marshall's first sermons was about not judging others. The next one was on gossip. We've never had too much trouble with either one, but we don't have *any* now. Besides, if somebody gives you trouble, Wade will hang them from the rafters by their thumbs."

Andi smiled in spite of her apprehension. "Hope you have a tall ladder."

Since Andi's first visit was bound to cause a stir, they had purposely arrived when church was scheduled to begin. Ray and Della were saving space for them, and they slipped into their seats as the song leader announced the number of the first hymn. Excited murmurs flew around the auditorium, a low hum not hidden by the scraping of the hymnals against the wooden racks as they were drawn from the backs of pews or the rustle of paper as the church members searched for the right page.

The book was new, but as Wade opened it to the first song, Andi was thankful to see it was an old hymn, "Standing on the Promises," with which she was familiar. According to Dawn, they still sang hymns each week, but also choruses and praise songs, many taken from popular contemporary Christian music. Dawn had taught her some of them, but Andi had worried that if they sang something she didn't know, people would realize how very long it had been since she had set foot inside a church building.

She relaxed slightly and sang the song from her heart, being careful, however, to moderate her voice so she didn't overwhelm those directly in front of her. She was surprised to discover how much of it she still knew from memory.

At the end of the song, the pastor told them to turn and greet one another. Miss Atkins and Mr. Garner sat directly in front of them. Andi almost did a double-take when the undertaker turned around to say hello. Dressed in his typical black suit, she expected the somber, cadaverous man she remembered. Instead, she encountered twinkling blue eyes and a genuinely warm smile. The man had also gained twenty or thirty pounds so he no longer looked like a walking skeleton.

"Andi, dear, it's so nice to see you," said her former school teacher. "You look as if you're feeling much better."

"I am. And it's nice to see you, too." Andi greeted Mr. Garner, then was gently nudged by Wade, who introduced her to the young couple and their small daughter sitting behind them.

As the congregation resumed their seats, the pastor asked if anyone had met someone new. A couple on the other side of the church were introduced, and one of the high school kids had brought a friend. They were greeted by warm applause. Andi was thinking how much she liked this new informality, when she heard the pastor ask Dawn if she would like to introduce her cousin. Dawn had warned her this would probably happen, and that it would be appropriate for her to greet the congregation if she wanted to. She suddenly realized how much she wanted to thank them for their prayers, even though she was still nervous about what kind of reception they might give her.

"I understand that to many of you, this lady is not a stranger," said the pastor. "But some of us have not yet had the privilege of meeting her, only praying for her."

Wade covered her hand with his. Strength and peace flowed through her, and she once again thought how right it would be to always have this man by her side.

Dawn stood up and took the cordless microphone that a young man handed to her. "As most of you know, I received a call several weeks ago that my cousin, Andi Carson, had been rushed to the hospital." Mist filled her eyes, and she cleared her throat. "Her friend asked me to pray, and to ask others to pray, because the doctors weren't sure if she was going to make it."

Andi heard Wade's sharp intake of breath as his grip tightened painfully on her hand. She glanced up at him, meeting hurt and accusation in his gaze. She leaned toward him, and he lowered his head so she could whisper in his ear. "I didn't know these details until late last night. They only told me that they had been worried." He loosened his hold, but still kept her hand clasped firmly in his.

"I called the prayer chain," said Dawn, "and you got busy. You not only prayed, but you called friends in other churches and asked them to pray. For almost eighteen hours, we didn't know if Andi was going to live or die. God was gracious and heard our prayers." Dawn's smile lit up her face. "And he even added a special treat by letting her come stay with me while she mends completely. So, now that I've stolen all her thunder, I'd like you to welcome my cousin, Andrea Carson."

Wade gave Andi's hand a tiny squeeze and released it before she stood on shaking legs. She was greeted by enthusiastic applause as she took the microphone from Dawn and smiled at the others in the sanctuary. "Thank goodness Dawn warned me she might do this." Hearing a few chuckles, she let her gaze drift around the room. "I see many people I knew in this church as I was growing up, people I know prayed for me when I was ill. I also see many faces I don't recognize, but I understand you were praying, too. I want to thank each of you from the bottom of my heart."

She paused, collecting her thoughts, intending to end quickly and sit down. Her gaze landed on two rows of teenagers sitting at the front. Not one of them fidgeted; no one looked bored. They were hanging onto her every word, some with tears rolling down their cheeks. It hit her that Wade and Dawn had been right. She had an opportunity to make a difference if she had the courage to be honest about her life and her renewed faith. In that moment, she understood that everything that had happened to her—both good and bad—had been for a purpose. Her belief in Jesus was not only to be shared in quiet times with individuals but publicly as the Lord led.

Uncertain as to what she should do, she looked at the pastor. He smiled kindly and nodded. "Go ahead, Andi. I believe the Lord has something he wants you to share this morning. We're not bound by a strict schedule, as long as we don't forget to take the offering," he added with a mischievous grin.

Several people laughed, and Andi felt some of the tension drain away. She turned back to the youngsters, her gaze lingering on one young girl. "I accepted the Lord as my Savior when I was just about your age. He was very real to me, a close, dear friend." She scanned the row as she talked, looking directly at each boy and girl. "But when I went off to seek my way in the world, I slowly left Jesus behind. There wasn't a specific time when I decided I didn't want to live for him anymore; I just drifted away. Life got busy, and I didn't think I had time to go to church. I quit reading my Bible, and gradually even stopped praying.

"It took several years, but I worked hard, concentrating only on my career, and finally achieved the success I had dreamed of. I became famous, at least with the millions of people who enjoy country music. But do you know what I discovered?" Several of the young people shook their heads, and not one of them looked away. She sensed that she also had the attention of every other person in the room, except possibly for the young mother who was carrying her fussy baby to the foyer.

"I wasn't even as happy as I'd been in high school. There was this great big emptiness inside, and I couldn't figure out why. I must be pretty dense, because God had to let me get so sick I almost died before I would slow down and take time to listen."

Her gaze skimmed over the faces in the crowd and found no condemnation. "He used two very wise, dear people to talk to me." She glanced at Dawn and Wade. "They helped me realize that I could never be whole without God's love and peace in my heart, that I needed his joy to find happiness. They also helped me to see that I couldn't let my feelings of guilt stand between me and Jesus, that he forgives us and sets our feet back on the right path with loving kindness. He has been watching over me all along, protecting me in ways that I'm only now beginning to understand.

"I'm not quite well, but I'm getting better every day. I want to serve the Lord in whatever way he wants. You folks helped save my life, so I'm going to be selfish and ask you to keep praying for me for a while, to ask him to clearly show me that direction." She turned toward the pastor, murmuring her thanks, and handed the microphone back to the young man who had brought it to them.

She sat down, and the minister thanked her for sharing, but Andi barely heard him. As she slid back against the pew, Wade put his arm around her and hugged her close—right there in front of everybody.

ஓை

That afternoon, Andi reclined lazily in an outdoor lounge chair in Wade's back yard. Dawn and Della sat at the picnic table looking at a new book on antique snuff boxes that Della had found on a recent trip to Houston. Ray sat near Andi, playing with one of the hired hand's cats by trailing a piece of twine along the ground until the animal caught it. The big orange tabby had sauntered in a few minutes after the scent of frying fish filled the air.

Andi watched Wade expertly roll another fillet of catfish in the cornmeal and drop it into the wire mesh fryer basket with three other pieces. He lowered the basket into the deep fryer filled with hot oil, making this the seventh or eighth batch of fish he had cooked since their arrival. He had a metal table set up as a cooking area on the patio with a single gas burner fueled from a special tank.

After his various comments downplaying his ability in the kitchen, she was surprised to learn he actually did the cooking. Taking her first bite, she instantly decided he had fish-frying down to an art, and his tossed green salad was excellent.

Struggling, she awkwardly pushed herself up out of the recumbent lawn chair. "No way to get out of one of these things gracefully," she said when Ray grinned.

"Not unless you've got real long legs." He tossed the cat a bite of fish and laughed as the animal hopped up on the vacant chair. "Or if you're a feline."

She strolled over beside Wade. "How much are you going to cook?"

"As much as anybody wants." His smile held more than a trace of satisfaction. "Something tells me you like catfish."

"I like this. I've never had fish of any kind that tasted this good."

He puffed out his chest. "Must be the cook. It also helps to eat it as it comes out of the cooker." He looked around, first at the low, grassy hill behind the house, then up at a single cloud, turning orange from the setting sun. "And it helps to be outside and in good company." He motioned to several of the cooked pieces on a plate beside the cooker. "Those should be cool enough to eat by now."

"No more for me. I'm stuffed."

He turned to the others. "There's more fish over here if you want it."

Dawn and his aunt shook their heads, but Ray meandered over and picked up a piece. He quickly dropped it back on the plate. "That one's got the directions still on it." He winked at Andi. "Says 'put me down.' "

"Sorry, I thought they'd cooled off enough."

"It's close. I just need something to set it on." He returned a few seconds later with his paper plate and helped himself to two more pieces.

"You're going to have some left over." Andi peeked in the bubbling oil where the fish was turning a crisp, golden brown.

"Not as much as you think. I got behind on my eatin'."

"Oh, poor baby. Hard to eat and cook, too?"

He nodded. "It's a big sacrifice."

She gingerly touched a cooked fillet with her fingers. "This one is cool enough. Open wide." She lifted the fish to his mouth. He bit off a big chunk, then quickly sucked in air. "Too hot?"

He shook his head, his eyes twinkling as he swallowed. "Best fish I ever tasted."

"Must be the one serving it."

"Must be. Tastes as sweet as sugar."

"Yuk. I don't think sugar-coated fish would be very good."

He laughed. "Probably not." He opened his mouth again, and she popped the rest of the fish inside it. After he ate the bite, he asked, "Shouldn't you be feeding me grapes?"

"Sorry. I didn't see any in your refrigerator."

Wade took the last of the fish fillets out of the pan and set them on a thick layer of paper towels to drain, then turned off the burner and closed the valve on the tank.

"This is a nice set up. Do you use it often?" *Do you cook like this for other women?* She met his gaze, striving for a disinterested expression, suspecting she failed miserably.

"Not too often. Mostly for family or some of the folks from church. I've occasionally repaid a few dinners this way." A faint glimmer lit his eyes. "Would you get the door for me? I need to go wash this cornmeal and fish off my hands."

"Sure." Andi walked over and opened the screen door, trying to ignore a stab of disappointment. It was ridiculous to be hurt because he had entertained other women in his home.

"Want to come help?" he asked, wiggling his eyebrows in a barely-recognizable Groucho Marx imitation.

She laughed and followed him through the doorway. She leaned against the counter as he washed his hands with soap, then splashed them with lemon juice to help take away the fishy smell. Reaching for a towel, Wade said quietly, "I like having you here, Andi."

"And I like being here," she replied softly.

Dawn came bustling into the kitchen, carrying the plate of fish and what was left of the salad. "Oops. Looks like my timing was way off." She set the dishes on the counter and made a bee-line for the back door. "Ray and Della are heading home before it gets too dark to see the ruts in the road. I'm going to walk down with them and look at some stuff she found last weekend. Pick me up when you're ready to leave." She paused long enough to take a breath, adding with exaggerated nonchalance, "Take your time."

As the back screen door slammed, Wade and Andi both glanced out the window. A turtle could have trudged the distance to Ray and Della's place before dark. They looked at each other and grinned.

"We have real subtle relatives, don't we?" He threw the towel on the counter and closed the small distance between them. "Of course, they've probably known all day that I've been waiting to get you alone." He put his arms around her, drawing her close.

"You have?" She looped her arms around his neck and batted her eyelashes a la Scarlett O'Hara. "My goodness, whatever for?"

"For this." He feathered a tiny kiss at the corner of her lips. "And this...."

Several moments later, he lifted his head. "Want to go sit on the porch swing and listen to the crickets sing?"

"Sounds like a line from a country song." She leaned her forehead against his chin and wondered if she were capable of walking anywhere after his kiss had made her toes curl.

"Maybe we'll come up with a hit."

Honey, I think we already have. She had to bite her tongue to keep from saying the words out loud. "It's a good start."

They walked out to the front porch, laughing as the swing swayed precariously when they sat down. Andi grabbed hold of the side until they were balanced. "Now, I understand why parents used to let their daughters sit out on the swing with their beaus."

Wade pushed his foot against the porch, gently setting the swing into motion as he put his arm around her. "They knew the poor wretch would dump them both out if he got too carried away. Warm enough?"

"Yes." She leaned her head on his shoulder and sighed softly.

"What's wrong?"

"Nothing. That was the sound of pure contentment. This is nice."

"Yes, it is." He rested his cheek against the top of her head. "Written any more songs this week?"

"I played with one yesterday, but it's not right yet. Actually it's a little low for me, but I think it might be a good one for Nicki. I suspect she's stronger on the lower notes than I am."

"Maybe you could do a duet."

"I hadn't thought of that, but it should work. We'll have to give it a try tomorrow."

"You're really looking forward to working with her, aren't you?" He sounded as if it surprised him.

And why shouldn't it? It surprised her. "Yes, I am. Two or three months ago, I don't think I would have been interested. More likely, I would have considered her a threat."

"And you don't now?"

"She'll be competition, but it doesn't bother me. My career isn't the most important thing in my life anymore. If God wants me to stay where I am, he will bless my efforts. If not, he will open other doors."

"You aren't seriously thinking about quitting, are you?" He looked down at her, concern and disbelief etched in his frown.

She shook her head, mindful that she would never want to

quit completely. "Making music is like breathing to me."

"You have such a gift, Andi. So many are blessed by your music. And now that you're walking with the Lord again, you have a tremendous chance to share his love with others, with people who might never hear about him otherwise."

"I know, and I want to do it. But sometimes I almost wish I couldn't carry a tune."

"Don't even think that."

"I said almost. I know God has blessed me, and I thank him for it, but there are other things I want, things that would be difficult with my career."

"Such as?"

She felt him tense and sensed his withdrawal even though he didn't physically move away. Considering how his mother had treated him, she doubted she could easily convince him that loving him was so important to her. She had to be patient. In time, he would see how much he meant to her. "Oh, I have a whole list. I haven't sorted through it all."

She walked her fingers across his lower ribs and hugged him. His tension seemed to evaporate. "Sitting here with you rates pretty high. Of course, that could be because I'm too full to move." She patted his stomach. "You had more fish than I thought you did."

"Are you saying I'm getting fat?"

"That's stretching it. I just meant your tummy doesn't sound like an empty oil drum."

He laughed. "I'm not sure whether I've been insulted or complimented."

"Neither one. 'Twas only an observation. I've gained four

pounds, which is good. Probably ten after tonight, which is all I need to gain back. Actually, I'd like to have a big belly someday," she said wistfully. "The kind that goes away after nine months."

"Then you get to lug the weight around on one hip. Kinda puts a hitch in your walk." Even though he was teasing her, his voice held a tender, affectionate note. She thought—or was she only hoping—she heard longing there, too.

Wanting to end the line of conversation, she faked a yawn. She hadn't intended to start talking about babies. "I'd better go. Dawn has to meet a man at her store early in the morning for a quote on the new heating and cooling system."

After retrieving Andi's purse and his keys from the house, Wade gave her a quick rundown on all the switches and gismos on the Blazer.

"Maybe I should have asked to borrow the roadster," said Andi, teasing him. "It doesn't have so many things for me to break."

"Sorry, but you can't drive it."

"Well, thanks a bunch."

He leaned against the side of the Blazer, close to the open window. "I didn't say I wouldn't let you drive it. I said you can't. You're too short. The seat is custom built to fit me, and it doesn't move up. Guess you'll just have to get a roadster of your own and have it customized to fit you."

"I might do that. I've always wanted a white one with red and orange flames on the side."

He laughed and straightened as she started the Blazer. "That sounds like your style. I'll be on the lookout for something."

"I won't buy anything that doesn't meet with your personal

approval. I want on-sight inspection."

"That may be hard if you find something in Nashville or while you're on tour."

"Ever heard of an airplane? Marvelous invention."

"So you're telling me that if you find something in Humptulips, Washington, you expect me to fly up there and check it out?"

"I don't know. I've never heard of it. Can you get there from here?"

He smiled. "Probably not. But I reckon I'd give it a try, seein' as how I like old cars."

"Now I'm jealous of a car." She put the Blazer into reverse, creeping backward.

"Darlin', by the time I got there, you'd be some place else."

"Oh, I don't know." She smiled, letting her love shine in her eyes, although she doubted he could see it in the dim light. "For you, I might stay around." She changed gears and pulled away slowly, waving goodbye and muttering to herself. "And I'm not talking about Humptulips, Washington. I'm talkin' about Buckley, Texas. Figure it out, you big, lovable yahoo."

Twelve

❧

R un through that last phrase again. I'm missing a chord in there somewhere." Andi listened carefully as Nicki played the guitar and sang the last line of a song she had written. "Okay, let's try it." Nicki began the phrase, and Andi accompanied her with the piano part she had composed after first hearing the song.

"That's it!" cried Nicki, barely taking a breath after ending the last note. "Andi, that makes it absolutely beautiful."

"Not bad, if I do say so myself, although it was already beautiful. It will sound even better with a bass and drums. A good keyboardist may add sounds neither of us has thought of. You'll be surprised when you get in a jam session with the band and they start improvising."

"Is it really going to happen? Am I going to Nashville?" Nicki's expression was hopeful yet incredulous.

Andi laughed. "Yes, kiddo. Dreams and reality are colliding. Kyle is practically pacing the floor waiting for this tape. He wants us to send it express, so he can get it tomorrow. Now, are you ready to record this one?"

"Yes, ma'am." Nicki immediately settled down, placed her fingers on the strings, and focused on the music.

Andi nodded at Dawn to start the tape recorder, then she began the introduction she had added to the poignant ballad of a woman yearning for the man she loved. Nicki came in, her fingers light and precise on the strings of the guitar, her voice strong but husky with an emotional intensity that had not been present a few minutes earlier. Her voice gradually rose majestically, then fell to a hushed whisper by the end of the song. The last notes, slowly played in the high octaves on the piano, lingered in the air like the lonesome call of a whippoorwill.

Andi blinked back tears as she lifted her fingers from the keys, aching to be in Wade's arms. If the song had this kind of impact when she was only minutes away from him, what would she do when she was clear across the country? How could she hear it at every show and still walk out on stage?

She didn't think she had ever heard a more tender love song, nor one sung with more honest, heart-wrenching emotion. If her instincts were right—and they were seldom wrong when it came to music and the music business—this song would be Nicki's first single, and it would take her to the top of the charts.

Dawn stopped the tape recorder and sniffed loudly, wiping her eyes with a tissue. "That was beautiful. It had to be written with someone special in mind."

Nicki took a deep breath, releasing it slowly. "I wrote it about a year ago, after my boyfriend and I broke up. He went off to the Navy and didn't want to be tied down. It was the right thing to do, but I still miss him when I sing it."

"Using your emotions sometimes plays a big part in turning a good song into a great one, but it's not easy. You'll find that it helps to follow a heart-tugger with something lively and happy," said Andi. She stretched her arms over her head and glanced at the clock. "Let's take a break. Then we'll do that sassy thing you were showing me this morning. If we put it on the tape next, Kyle will go nuts. He won't be able to get you on a plane fast enough."

"Please don't pinch me or wake me up," said Nicki with a laugh.

They took some pop from the refrigerator and went out on the back porch for about fifteen minutes. When they went back to work, Nicki was relaxed and playful, getting downright spunky on the last song.

Laughing, Andi twirled halfway around on the piano stool, waved her hands in the air, and stomped her feet. "I've created a monster! If I take you on tour, the audience will boo me off the stage." She looked at Dawn and cupped her hand behind her ear. "Do you hear it?"

Dawn grinned and played along. "I think so." She tilted her head and put her hand behind her ear, too. "Yes, the cry is faint but growing—Nicki, Nicki, Nicki! Boo, Andi! Go back to the bus!"

Nicki collapsed on the couch. "Y'all cut it out. That's never gonna happen."

"Well, hopefully not the booing part. Do you feel up to playing around with one more song? I've been working on one that I want you to try."

Nicki sat up, her face glowing. "You wrote a song for me?"

"Actually, it's for both of us. When it popped into my head, I decided you'd have to sing it because it was a little low for me. Then Wade suggested that I sing high harmony and make it a duet. It evolved from there." Nicki jumped up and hurried over to stand beside her. "I'll play it through so you can see how it goes," said Andi. "I was in a hurry when I scored it, but I think you can follow along."

They worked on the song for several minutes, stopping several times to smooth out timing and harmony variations. "Let's try it again. I think we've taken care of the trouble spots." Nicki sang with strength and clarity. Andi's voice rang out high and true. When their parts joined, it was as if God had ordained it. Their voices blended in magical perfection, with Nicki laying a velvet foundation of feeling, and Andi soaring to the heavens with sweetness and purity. When the song ended, neither of them could say anything. They simply looked at each other in amazement.

"That'll get the dogs out from under the porch!" cried Dawn, hopping up from her chair and rubbing her arms. "You gave me goose bumps. Are you going to put that one on the tape for Kyle?"

"No, we're going to do this one live," Andi said quietly.

As Andi predicted, Kyle called right after he heard the tape. "You say you found this kid at the shopping mall?"

"Actually, she found me," Andi replied with a laugh. "She came over and asked for my autograph."

"But, Andi, how did you know she could sing? Did she just belt out a song right there?"

"That would have been interesting. The only way I can explain it is to say God must have revealed it to me. There was something in her voice that caught my attention, and somehow, I knew, without any doubt, that she was a singer, and that I was supposed to help her."

"That's even wilder than if she started singing in the middle of the mall, but I'm glad you followed up on your intuition. She's dynamite. Can she fly out tonight?"

"Give the girl time to pack a suitcase—and tell her boss she's leavin' town. How about two days?"

"I knew you'd say that. All right, we'll plan for Thursday. I'll have Nadine make all the arrangements. Her tickets will be waiting for her at the airport in Sidell. We'll pick her up here in Nashville. Call and tell her the news, so she gets the screaming over with before I call. I'll give you ten minutes. I have a dinner meeting I can't miss, and I want to talk to her before I leave."

"Yes, sir. And Kyle…"

"Yes?"

"Mellow out a little, or you'll scare the poor girl to death. She doesn't know anything about barracudas yet."

"I'm not a barracuda. Just a little intense."

"That's an oxymoron. Besides, you're a lot intense. She's sweet and innocent, Kyle. Help her stay that way."

"Not street-wise like you were when I met you, huh?"

"Nope. She's nineteen but she still lives at home with her big, loving family. Take care of her, okay?"

"Anything for you. I'll treat her like my sister."

Andi laughed. "You may change your mind when you see her."

"Oh? What does she look like?"

"About five feet seven, probably a size ten, long blond hair and beautiful green eyes. She's very pretty. And sweet and innocent."

"You said that already. I promise I'll be on my best behavior—no lechery and no yelling."

"I'm going to hold you to that. And Kyle…"

"What?" His slightly-raised voice held more than a hint of impatience.

She pictured him shoving a note or a file at his secretary, and probably nodding or shaking his head at something the woman asked him. The man was destined for a heart attack before he reached forty. "Thanks. You're being a real doll about this."

"That's me. A big soft teddy bear."

Andi glanced at the bear Wade had given her and smiled. There was absolutely no comparison between the two men, although they were both dear to her in different ways. "Not even close. Now, slow down and take care of yourself, or you'll wind up sick, too. Did you eat lunch?"

"Don't remember," he replied absently.

She'd lost him. He probably had another phone pressed to his other ear. "Bye, super manager."

"Bye, hon."

She called Nicki, laughing as the girl screamed and the phone crashed to the floor. When Nicki picked it up, Andi quickly relayed what Kyle had said and told Nicki to call her if she had any questions.

Half an hour later, Nicki called back. "Andi, he was so nice. He doesn't sound at all like you've described him. He was very patient and encouraging. He said 'please' and 'thank you' and asked politely instead of issuing orders like you said he usually does."

"Amazing. Well, don't expect it to last. The man only has one speed—fast forward. He wants everything done immediately, if not sooner."

"But you like him don't you?"

"I adore Kyle." Andi looked up to see Wade scowling at her through the screen door. She smiled and motioned for him to come inside. "He's a good friend and one of the best managers in the business, but he goes through life like a runaway freight train. You may have to put on the brakes, or he'll have you working twenty-four hours a day. I keep telling him not everyone can function on three or four hours of sleep like he does."

Nicki groaned. "I need at least six or I'm incoherent."

"Then insist on it right from the start." Andi patted the couch beside her. Wade hooked his hat on the coat rack and ran his fingers through his hair. When he sat down, he was still wearing a frown. "Kyle respects people who stand up for themselves. But don't throw a fit, or he'll send you home. I've seen him do it more than once. Came close myself a couple of times at the beginning. Hold your ground, firmly but quietly."

"I don't yell much. Except when I'm excited."

"That's allowed. Oh, I forgot to tell you that Kyle is an extremely good-looking man, so don't be bowled over when you meet him."

"How handsome?"

"As good as any movie star you ever saw."

Nicki took a deep breath and released it slowly. "All right. Andi, what should I wear? I've never been on a plane before."

Andi slid her hand around Wade's arm, then stretched up and kissed him on the cheek. She grinned at his surprised expression and the slow smile that followed. "Wear jeans or something comfortable and take a sweater. Be sure to wear comfortable walking shoes. The Dallas airport is gigantic, and, as Wade's Uncle Ray put it, it's a real wasp nest—zillions of people going every which way. Don't be afraid to ask someone from the airlines to help you find your way around. Kyle will have someone pick you up in Nashville."

"He said the driver would hold up a sign with my name on it."

"That's the way it works. He may take you to a hotel when he picks you up from the airport, or he may take you directly to see Kyle. It won't matter if you go directly and are still dressed casually. He flies a lot so he will understand. Take some nice dresses and slacks, like you would wear to work or to church, and plenty of comfortable, casual things. The rehearsals are laid back. Nobody dresses up. If you have a question about what to wear, ask Kyle or his secretary, Nadine. She's a sweetie and will be a big help. Anything else?"

"Not right now. I'll probably think of something later. I can't believe I'm flying to Nashville! Andi, I don't know how to thank you."

"You're doing a good job of it. Just hang on tight, kid. It's going to be quite a ride. Now, go pack. The handsomest man in Texas just came through the door, and I haven't given him a proper welcome."

Nicki laughed softly. "Tell Wade hi for me, too."

Andi hung up the phone and smiled. "Nicki said hello."

He made an incoherent sound in this throat.

"What's the matter?"

He frowned and looked away, glaring out at the yard through the screen door. "I never asked if Kyle is married."

"No, he's not. The man doesn't have time for a wife. He's married to his job."

"But you still 'adore him.' Easy to do, I guess, since he looks like a 'movie star.' "

Her heart soared. He was jealous! She turned slightly, resting her hand on his chest. "He is handsome, but men in five-hundred-dollar-suits don't do much for me."

"Oh, really?" He didn't sound the least bit convinced.

Andi glanced at his clothes and nodded. "It takes a man in boots and jeans and a sky-blue western shirt to set my heart a-flutter."

A light flared in Wade's eyes as he looked down at her. "A-flutter, huh?"

"Flittin' all over the place."

"So, will any old cowboy in a blue shirt do?"

"Nope. He has to have light brown hair and gorgeous hazel eyes. And he has to be sitting next to me right this second."

"So what was this about a proper welcome?" he murmured, lowering his head toward hers, kissing her deeply.

When she could speak, she rested her head on his chest. "That was good enough to make me send you outside, so you can come back in again."

He put his arm around her. "Let's don't and say we did." He cradled her chin in his other hand, urging her to lift her head. When she did, he kissed her again and again…each time more passionately than the last until he slowly straightened and drew in a shaky breath. "You'd better open all the doors and windows and turn on the fan, darlin'. I think we're about to go up in smoke."

She smiled dreamily up at him. "What a way to go."

He chuckled softly. "I dropped by to ask—"

"You mean you had another reason?" She grinned impishly, enjoying the way his gaze focused briefly on her dimples.

"Right now, I'm not sure if I did or not." He paused, slanting his eyes upward as if concentrating took great effort. "Now I remember. I wanted to see if you would like to come out to the ranch on Thursday afternoon. Grant is going to be working some of the horses, and I thought you might enjoy watching him."

"I'd rather watch you."

A broad smile spread across his face. "Well, that can be arranged, but I might be cleaning out the stalls."

"On second thought, I've always wanted to see cutting horses at work. What time?"

"He's supposed to come out around one-thirty." Mischief glinted in his eyes. "You might want to arrive a few minutes early. I'll be busy once he gets there." He glanced at his watch. "I hate to, but I've got to run."

She made a point of looking at his cowboy boots. "That I gotta see."

"Figure of speech, sugar. I'm due at Clint's in five minutes." At her questioning look, he said, "Pastor Marshall to strangers in town."

"I'm not a stranger. I just forgot his first name."

"He's cookin' dinner. Deli chicken from Greene's Grocery."

She walked to the door with him. "Call me later?"

"I will if I get home before ten-thirty. After that, you'll have to wait until tomorrow. I need my beauty sleep."

"It must be working."

He smiled and kissed her slowly and thoroughly. "This keeps gettin' better and better."

160

"You thought it might get dull and boring?"

He grinned. "No, but I did think things might settle down once the new wore off."

"Not a chance." Andi put her arms around his neck and stretched up on tiptoe, kissing him with all the love in her heart. When she finally broke away and lowered her heels to the floor, she smiled at his stunned expression. "What we have isn't ever going to settle down," she said softly.

"Andi..." He looked completely dumbfounded.

She put her fingers to his lips. "Shhh. You don't want to be late. Go on to Clint's. Give him my best."

In a daze, he picked up his hat and put it on backward.

"Uh, Wade, honey, I think you need to turn your hat around."

He obeyed without a word, moving toward the door.

"Can you drive?"

"Been drivin' since I was eleven," he said absently, opening the screen door with a mighty shove. He walked down the porch steps, but when he reached the sidewalk, he turned around, staring at her.

She put on her most innocent expression. "Bye, sugar."

"Bye." He spun on his heel and walked swiftly to his pickup without another word.

When the telephone rang about nine-thirty, Dawn answered. A minute later, she hung up, shaking her head. "That was weird."

"Was it Wade?" asked Andi, racing in from the back porch

steps where she had been star gazing and praying.

Dawn nodded. "He said to tell you he made it home safely. I asked if he wanted to talk to you, but he said, 'Not tonight.' Did you two have a fight?"

A chill spread through her, and Andi shook her head. "No, but I think I made a big mistake."

Thirteen

❦

On Thursday afternoon, Wade sat on the top rail of the corral fence. He usually enjoyed watching Grant Adams work cattle with a cutting horse, but this time his heart wasn't in it.

Grant moved as one with the animal, guiding with a gentle nudge of a spur or the pressure of his knee now and then as the horse shifted back and forth, blocking the cow's desperate maneuvers to get back to the herd. The horse did most of the work, using her own natural instincts, but something about Grant seemed to bring out the best in her. She worked well for Wade, but he had found that most of his cutting horses did better after a few hours training with his friend.

Grant leaned forward and patted the horse on the neck, then guided her toward Wade, letting the cow run back to the herd. "Sadie's doin' better every time I come by. She must be getting plenty of practice."

"I try to work with her and Joe a couple of times a week. She still gets excited occasionally and messes up."

Grant smiled and patted the horse again. "She's young and spirited. She'll learn." He straightened and took off his hat, wiping his sweaty forehead on his light-weight denim shirt sleeve. "Too bad your lady friend couldn't make it. I was lookin' forward to the surprise. You gonna tell me who she is, or do I have to keep waitin'?"

Wade jumped down off the fence, guilt weighing heavily on his mind. He hadn't talked to Andi since Tuesday evening, since she hog-tied his brain and branded his heart and soul. She had left a message on his answering machine shortly before noon saying she couldn't make it because her doctor's appointment had been changed, and she had to go to Sidell today. That may have been true, but he figured she would have rescheduled it if he'd had the gumption to talk to her. Trouble was, he didn't know what to say.

Grant dismounted and led the horse, following Wade to the horse corral. "You look like you're up to your armpits in alligators and can't find the drain to the swamp."

"Andi Carson."

"Ride over that trail again," said Grant with a perplexed frown.

"My lady friend is Andi Carson, the country singer."

Grant whistled softly. "How did an ugly cuss like you meet up with a woman like her?"

Wade managed a halfhearted smile. "We were friends in high school. She's been sick and is staying with her cousin while she recovers." He unfastened the saddle, tugging it and the saddle blanket from the horse.

Grant led Sadie over to the water trough and slipped off the bridle. He followed Wade to the tack room, waiting outside as he put away the saddle, then handed him the bridle. "Looks to me like what you're feelin' is a heap more than friendship."

Wade sighed and shut the door to the tack room, watching the horse roll in the dirt for a minute before heading for the corral gate. He noticed that Grant was limping. "Your knee botherin' you?"

"Yeah. Must be a cool front coming in." They stopped at Grant's pickup, where he unfastened his spurs and tossed them into a box in the back. "Now what's the story?" he asked as they walked slowly toward the house.

"I've never told another soul this, Grant, so I'd appreciate it if you keep it under your hat." When his friend gave him a curt nod, Wade continued. "I met Andi when I moved here my senior year. I fell for her the first time I saw her."

"She's a pretty lady, that's a fact."

"I never let on to anybody how I felt. Especially Andi. I knew she wouldn't stay around Buckley. I thought I'd gotten over her, but as soon as I saw her again, I realized I hadn't. We've spent a lot of time together since she's been back, and now I know I'll never love anybody else." They stopped in the kitchen, grabbing a couple of cans of pop, then went into the living room.

When Wade motioned for Grant to take the recliner, he sat down, leaned back, and put his feet up with a heartfelt sigh. "You may never get me out of this thing. If I start snorin', let me be. So what about Andi? Are you more than just a passin' fancy?"

Wade sprawled on the couch, resting his feet on the rugged coffee table. "I think maybe I am."

About to take a drink of grape soda, Grant paused and pierced Wade with his gaze. "You mean the lady is in love with you?"

"I think so." He leaned his head against the back of the couch with a groan. "I don't know if she really is or just thinks she is."

165

"Either way, it's a problem."

"She'll be leaving before long. The doctor is probably going to give her the go-ahead today. Andi and I live in two different worlds. I can't live in hers, and I can't ask her to give it all up and live in mine. She's worked too hard and loves it too much."

Grant was silent for a few minutes, regret mirrored in his eyes. "I can't see you wanderin' around the country in a bus, playin' Mr. Andi Carson."

"I couldn't do it. Maybe now and then, but not all the time."

"And being apart so much can ruin a marriage," Grant said bitterly.

Wade knew his friend spoke from first-hand experience. Grant had paid a high price to follow the rodeo. "I couldn't stand being here and having her on the road, either. I'd go out of my mind worrying about her, worrying about what might happen—knowing all the things that could happen."

"Loneliness and temptation. One way or the other, the trap usually gets sprung." They sat quietly for a while, each lost in his own thoughts. Finally, Grant looked at Wade. "So what are you going to do?"

"I don't know. I've prayed and prayed and still don't have an answer."

"You really expected one? Haven't you figured out that the Man Upstairs—if there really is one—doesn't answer prayers?"

Wade's heart went out to his friend. Grant had made his mistakes, but he had been deeply hurt, too. "He's there, and he answers prayer. Sometimes, he just doesn't answer the way we want him to."

"Then why bother to pray at all?"

"Because in the end, his way is the right way."

Grant flipped the lever to lower the footrest on the recliner. He slowly pushed himself up out of the chair, grimacing in pain. "I'd better go. Got chores to do before dark."

Wade didn't argue or try to talk any more about spiritual matters. Until his friend was ready to hear more, all Wade could do was pray and sow a few seeds. "Don't wait so long to come back. We don't always have to work."

Grant snorted. "Ain't got time to play. Don't remember how, anyway." He grabbed his hat and limped out the door, heading toward the corrals and his pickup.

Wade stretched out in the recliner, thinking seriously about a nap. He hadn't slept worth a hoot for a couple of nights. About the time he got comfortable, the doorbell rang. The door was open, so he wasn't surprised to hear the screen door creak.

"Anybody home? Wade? Andi? Anybody here?"

"Come on in, Dawn." Wade got up, only taking two steps before Dawn bustled into the room. "Andi's not here."

"I thought she was coming out to spend the afternoon. That was the plan when I left this morning."

"She left a message on my machine that she was going to see the doctor today instead of tomorrow."

"Well, if you'd called her, she wouldn't have gone off in a huff."

"I had some things to work out."

"Did you get them resolved?"

"No. How is she?"

"Wondering what's going on in that pea-sized brain of yours, so get with the program and call her."

"Yes, ma'am." Wade let his gaze slowly drift over her. He'd seen Dawn in all kinds of outfits—from her Sunday best to her garden clothes—but he'd never seen her looking such a mess. She wore a bright orange T-shirt tucked into old, frayed jeans. Both were badly splattered with deep rose paint. He stepped closer. She had paint specks on her arms and face and a swipe of dark pink on the end of her nose. Rose splotches and streaks highlighted her blond curls, but she still looked cute. "Glad you got dressed up to come see me."

She waved away his comment and hurried into the kitchen portion of the big open room, talking ninety-miles-an-hour. "I'm going to bum some pop. I'm dying of thirst. Been painting the bathroom at the store and breathing the fumes all day." Her jeans sported a perfect rose-colored hand print beside the left hip pocket.

Wade grinned, barely refraining from laughing out loud. "Did you get any paint on the walls?"

Grant stepped through the front door, glanced at Wade, then focused on Dawn, who was digging around in the refrigerator.

"Yes, I did, smarty," she said. "It's impossible to use a roller without a little splattering."

Grant nudged the front brim of his hat up for a better view, then looked at Wade again and silently asked if this was Andi.

Wade shook his head, aware that from his angle, Grant couldn't see Dawn's blond hair. His friend looked surprised, then instantly curious, and turned his attention back to the woman who was half-hidden by the refrigerator door.

"Wade, don't you have any grape pop?" she asked, her voice muffled as she moved things around in the refrigerator. "Don't you ever clean this thing?"

"No, to both questions."

"All you've got left is cream soda." She shuddered delicately. "Can't stand the stuff. Ick!" She popped out of the refrigerator and tossed a half-wrapped chunk of fuzzy green cheese into the sink. "Branching out into pharmaceuticals?" Her upper body disappeared again inside the refrigerator. Seconds later a plastic bag flew into the sink. "That cucumber is swimming in slim. When did you cut it, a month ago?"

"Probably six."

She straightened, shut the refrigerator door, and started opening cabinets. "Guess I'll have to settle for water. Where are all your glasses?"

"In the dishwasher."

She shrugged gracefully. "Makes sense. Why bother to unload it when you know where everything is." As she zipped over to the dishwasher and plucked a glass from inside, Wade glanced at Grant. His friend stood transfixed, staring at Dawn with a mixture of amazement, bewilderment, and admiration.

"Did you have a special reason for trying to find Andi, or did you drop by to clean out my refrigerator?"

She took a long drink and refilled the glass from the tap. "Kyle needed to talk to her right away. I tried to phone, but no one answered, and I didn't know when you'd get around to checking your machine if I left a message. Besides, the last time I left a message on that thing, it cut me off before I said my name. I figured you were down at the corrals, and it would be better if I dashed out and told her in person. But that didn't work, since she's not here. Good thing I left her a note."

Wade glanced at Grant again. He was frowning and absently scratching the stubble on his jaw. "Why would you leave her a

169

note when you were coming out here to talk to her?"

"The way you two haven't been talking lately, I thought she might have already left. I might not meet her on my way out from town if she went some place else, and if she got home before I did, she could go ahead and call Kyle."

Wade met Grant's gaze with a smile. It made sense, in a Dawn sort of way. His buddy appeared to be trying to sort it all out.

She took another drink and glanced at the clock on the stove. "Grandpa's whiskers! Is your clock right?"

"Yep."

"I've got to go." She slammed the plastic glass down on the counter, knocking it over in her haste. "Drat!" Grabbing the dishrag from the back of the sink, she mopped up the water. "I have to be at the city council meeting in two hours, and I still have to bake cookies for the missionary bake sale and take them over to Velma's tonight."

She rushed out of the kitchen, drilling Wade with her gaze. "You are planning to take Andi to the dance next Friday, aren't you? Since word got out that she's singing a couple of songs, our tickets have been selling faster than popcorn at the county fair. But she won't feel like singing if you don't start behaving yourself. And she's going to throw a party for the townspeople and sign autographs at my store on Wednesday afternoon. We could use a few bodyguards to keep the screaming hordes in line. Call the woman and put her out of her misery. Better yet, go see her."

Dawn came to a screeching halt about a step-and-a-half shy of plowing right into Grant. He grabbed her upper arms to steady her. "Oh, excuse me!" Her face instantly turned scarlet, which clashed with the orange T-shirt and rose paint. "I didn't know Wade had company."

Wade observed his two friends with amusement. For a gal who supposedly had sworn off men, and a man who put women in the same category as rattlesnakes, they were sure staring at each other. He was astonished to see a tiny smile crease Grant's face as he slowly lowered his hands.

"What kind of car are you drivin', ma'am?"

"A blue Ford van. Why?"

"Does it have auto-pilot?"

Dawn laughed and shook her head. "No, but the road's straight. All I have to do is point it toward town."

"Glad I'm goin' the other direction." Grant's smile widened minutely. He touched the brim of his hat politely. "Grant Adams, ma'am."

"Dawn Carson. Andi's cousin, and occasionally Wade's friend." Her pointed look told Wade this might not be one of those occasions. "It's nice to meet you, and I'm glad I didn't run you down, but I really do have to go."

Grant stepped aside, allowing her to pass.

"Bye, Wade. Call Andi, will ya? I'm sick of hearing the blues." She dashed out the door at full speed, letting the screen slam behind her.

"Whew! Is she always like that?" Grant asked softly, staring out the front door.

Wade chuckled. "Pretty much. Dawn's a regular whirlwind."

Grant turned away from the door and shook his head, but a glimmer of admiration lingered in his eyes. "More like a three-ring circus."

"But a sweet one, and she's single. She'll be at the dance next Friday."

"But I won't be. I'm not interested, even if she is pretty."

"Why did you come back?"

"I thought I'd swipe another pop for the trip home." Grant started for the door.

"You can have the cream soda."

"Can't stand the stuff." Grant made a face and walked out the door, letting the screen slam behind him.

Fourteen

❧

Yes, Kyle, I know she's fantastic." Andi held the phone with one hand and pulled the flour canister out of the cabinet with the other, setting it beside the sugar container on the counter. After spotting Dawn's "to do" list, the cookie recipe, and four sticks of softened butter, she'd decided to help out with the baking. "Give her a chance to rest. I doubt if she slept at all last night, and she'd never flown before. She's probably a nervous wreck."

"I know." Kyle laughed softly. "She still blew me away when she sang, even though her hands were shaking so bad I was sure she'd hit the wrong string. Actually, she's curled up asleep on the couch in my office right now. I'm using Nadine's phone."

"Why Kyle, you do have a heart."

"Maybe." There was an odd note in his voice. "After she sleeps awhile, I'll buy her dinner and take her to the hotel so she can crash. We should be able to get rolling on Monday. Jake's lining up a backup band—already found a drummer and a bass player. He's auditioning a couple of keyboard guys tomorrow and has some calls out for a lead guitarist. When do you go back to the doctor?"

Andi measured a cup of sugar into the mixer bowl. "I saw him today. Everything is back to normal. He's released me."

"You coming back tomorrow or Saturday?"

"Not so fast, buster. I need more time. I promised Dawn I'd sing at a benefit dance next weekend."

"I can live with that."

"Can you try to hold things off even longer?"

"I'll try, but I may not be too successful. We don't have much option on most of the tentative dates. Are you still seeing Wade?"

"I haven't for a few days."

"But? What are you not telling me, hon?"

"I'm in love." She smiled at Kyle's groan. "And to be honest, I don't want to leave at all. I want to stay right here forever."

"Andi, you can't. You've got commitments. I have almost all the concerts rescheduled. And you've got another album to do before your contract is up."

She pictured him digging in his pocket for antacid tablets. "I know, and I intend to fulfill my obligations, but my career isn't the most important thing to me anymore. Don't get an ulcer yet; the big lug hasn't said anything about marriage."

"But he loves you?"

"I thought you didn't believe in love."

"We're talking about Wade, not me."

"He hasn't used words to say he's in love, but everything else he does tells me he is."

Kyle groaned again. "Why do I see my career—not to mention my fortune—evaporating?"

"That's one reason I sent Nicki to you," said Andi, realizing it was true. "You can take her to the top just like you did me. And I'm not going to fire you, nor do I want to quit completely. I just want to slow down."

"How much?"

"I haven't figured that part out yet. Actually, I think Wade is scared of the whole thing, so nothing may happen."

"Hi there," said Kyle softly, sounding as if he were no longer speaking directly into the phone.

Andi blinked, not only at his words, but at the tenderness with which they were uttered. The only time she had heard him speak so gently to anyone was when she woke up in the hospital.

"Do you feel better after your nap?"

Andi's mouth dropped open. Sinking down on a kitchen chair, she listened to Nicki's sleepy reply and his soft chuckle. Even his laugh sounded sweet.

"You'll be all right after some dinner and a good night's sleep. Andi's on the phone. Do you want to talk to her?"

Seconds later, Nicki came on the line. "Hi, Andi."

"Hi, kiddo. How are you?"

"Tired, but I made the trip okay. I didn't get sick on the plane or lost in Dallas."

"Good for you. Sounds like Kyle is being nice." She shook her head at the understatement.

"Yes, he is. He gave me a copy of his proposed contract and suggested I look over it tomorrow when I'm not so zonked. He thought I might want to read it to Dad before I sign."

"That's a good idea." *And an unusual display of patience and consideration from Kyle.* "Call me if you have any questions.

I'm sure it's basically a standard contract and fair, but it never hurts to ask."

"Thanks, I will." Nicki yawned. "Sorry. I'm really out of it. I'd better go wash my face and try to wake up. Kyle wants to talk to you again."

"Call me tomorrow. Collect." When Kyle took the receiver, she blasted him. "Okay, Wilson, what are you up to?"

"Nothing. Just mellowing out like you asked. I haven't yelled once."

"I bet you haven't. You also said you wouldn't be a lecher, remember?"

"I remember, and I'm not."

Andi had seen the man in action many times, and she deeply regretted letting Nicki go to Nashville alone. The girl didn't stand a chance. "Kyle…"

"Don't worry, Andi. I'll be on my best behavior. I'm not going to take advantage of her. Neither is anyone else if I can help it." His voice was quiet yet intense. "You have my word on it."

Andi relaxed. Kyle's word was his bond. He never broke it. "Well, don't sweep the kid off her feet."

"I think the opposite may be true. I'll talk to you in a few days. Gotta go. I've promised a pretty lady dinner at Happy Burger."

Andi laughed as she hung up the phone, wondering how long it had been since her manager had actually set foot in a burger joint. Power lunches in high-class restaurants were more his style, along with the heartburn that went with them. "I never expected this. Lord, please take care of them both and don't let either of them get hurt."

"Are you talking to yourself or praying?" Dawn burst through the front door, tossing her purse on the couch.

"Both. Kyle seems to be quite taken with Nicki, and I don't mean just as a singer."

Dawn's eyes widened. "The Kyle I know? Our sweet country kid is charming Mr. Sophisticated?"

"Right out of his socks. He's even taking her out for a hamburger."

Dawn whooped. "Oh, I wish I could see that. Do you think he will wear his expensive suit?"

"Probably, although she might convince him to take off his tie." Andi laughed and went back to the counter, dumping the butter in with the sugar. "Did you see Wade?" She turned on the mixer, thoroughly blending the two ingredients.

Dawn poured some chocolate chips from the package into her hand and leaned against the counter. "Thanks for taking care of the cookies." She rotated her head slowly, then each shoulder. "Yes, I saw him. He told me you had gone to Sidell. What did Doc have to say?"

"That I'm fine. Everything is back to normal. I'm free again. No more doctor visits. He wants me to have a blood count done in a month." Andi scraped the creamy mixture off the side of the bowl. "What else did Wade have to say?" She cracked two eggs and dumped them in, tossing the shells into the garbage.

"That he hadn't called because he has some things to work out. I think he may call tonight. He had dark circles under his eyes. I don't expect he's been sleeping, either."

"He isn't sick, is he?"

"Confused, yes. Sick, no. Ornery, definitely."

Andi set a cup of flour down on the counter, looking closely at her cousin for the first time since Dawn came home. "Good grief! Did you get any paint on the wall?"

Dawn glared at her. "That's what that no account boyfriend of yours said. And in front of Grant Adams, too, I expect." She rolled her eyes. "Oh, Andi, it was awful. I flew out there, looking like a thrift shop reject, and went digging through Wade's refrigerator, throwing things out and nagging him like a fishwife. When I realized how late it was, I dashed for the door and practically knocked him down."

"Wade?"

Dawn impatiently shook her head. "Grant Adams. The absolutely most perfect cowboy I've ever seen."

"Wade is the perfect cowboy."

"True, in a good-guy sort of way."

"And Grant is a bad-guy cowboy?" Andi crossed her arms. Dawn usually dated the polite, easy going, boy-next-door type.

"Well, I hope not really, but he made me think of an outlaw. Black hair, a little shaggy. Dark stubble, more like he just didn't bother to shave this morning than five o'clock shadow. Dusty jeans that were kinda worn, denim shirt, and a beat-up black hat, but he looked like a hard-working man, not a bum. Handsome in a rugged kind of way, with the most beautiful, vivid blue eyes I've ever seen. And he *did* hold me up," she added, her eyes twinkling.

"To keep you from falling, I suppose."

"Aw, quit being so sharp. He even smiled at me."

Andi went back to making the cookies. "That's not unusual. People smile at you all the time."

"I know, but I had the oddest feeling that he didn't want to but couldn't help it. And then he teased me. When I glanced at Wade, he was staring at Grant with his mouth open, totally amazed."

Andi laughed. "Obviously being covered in paint wasn't such a big deal. I thought you had given up on men."

"A passing phase." Dawn grinned. "I am trying to quit worrying about finding Mr. Right and let God take care of it. Chances are, I'll never see Grant Adams again, but it's still nice to meet someone interesting. Well, I'd better go chisel off this paint. If those good ol' boys down at City Hall see my pink hair, they'll think I've turned into a floozy and won't give us a cent. Are we having anything besides cookies for dinner?"

"How about my specialty? Microwave frozen entrees."

"Sounds delightful. I'll take the fake Chinese stuff."

By the time Dawn left for her meeting, taking a box of chocolate chip cookies to drop off along the way, Andi had begun to worry that her cousin was wrong, and that Wade wouldn't call. For the next hour, she sat curled up in the big yellow chair, morosely flipping television channels with the remote control. She finally settled on a nature show about penguins. When the phone rang, she swallowed a half-eaten bite of cookie and washed it down with a swig of milk.

Wade sounded relieved when she answered. "I thought you might have gone out."

"Where? To the city council meeting? I'd rather channel surf."

"Find anything interesting?"

"Penguins sliding on the ice, just like kids going down a snow-covered hill on inner tubes. Looked as if they were having just as much fun, too. And the shopping channel has an elegant, white brocade sofa cover for only three hundred dollars."

"Now, I need that. How did it go at the doctor's?"

"Everything is back to normal. I'm officially well."

"Good." He paused and cleared his throat. "So when will you be leaving?"

"Not until after the museum benefit, at least. I asked Kyle to delay things as long as he can." *Please take the hint.* "He knows I want to take Nicki on tour with me, so he's finding a band for her. She'll need some time to put together a show and rehearse."

"Dawn said you were throwing an autograph party on Wednesday."

"I want to thank everyone for being so kind and for respecting my privacy. I think practically everyone in town knew I was here, but not a soul bothered me."

"She said you needed bodyguards."

"The sheriff and a couple of deputies will be there, and I'm sure they'll do a good job. But I'd feel better if you were around."

"What time?"

"One to five. I know that's a long time when you have work to do."

"I'll be there. Maybe I'll see if Grant wants to come along."

"How did he like Dawn?"

Wade chuckled softly, and she instantly felt warm and cozy.

"I don't think he knew what to make of her. She was in rare form this afternoon, movin' faster than a six-legged jack rabbit. Looked kinda cute, though—speckles, pink striped hair, and all. He did say she was pretty, but that he wasn't interested. I think maybe he was, but I doubt if he'll act on it.

"He used to be married, but his wife couldn't handle him being gone so much with the rodeo. She hid it well, and he probably wasn't paying close enough attention, even though he was crazy about her. He didn't have a clue that anything was wrong until he came home early from a trip. The baby-sitter told him his wife was on a date. They separated, then Grant got hurt in the rodeo. They were still apart almost a year later when she died from an allergic reaction to a wasp sting."

"How awful. He has children?"

"A little girl. She's nine or ten and lives in San Angelo with his mother. He goes to see her every chance he gets. He's made some mistakes, but he's a good guy. He's had more than his share of hurt and needs God's peace. I tell him about the Lord whenever I have the opportunity, but I have to tread lightly. What did Dawn think of him?"

"That he'd make a perfect outlaw."

Wade laughed. "He could have played the part today, that's a fact. He doesn't look so scruffy when he's cleaned up."

"She seemed to like scruffy, but she doesn't expect him to call her. She was rather mortified by both her appearance and her behavior, but she was also encouraged because she met someone interesting."

"That's good." He was quiet for a moment. "Andi, I'm sorry I haven't called these past couple of days. I still want to take you to the dance."

"I want you to."

"I've missed you."

"I've missed you, too. How about coming over for home-made pizza tomorrow evening?"

"I'd like to, but I have to go to Lubbock early tomorrow afternoon. Looks like I'll be gone all weekend. My dad called last night and asked me to help with a surprise birthday party for my grandpa. He's eight-five on Monday. I had been thinking about going up to see him on Sunday, but Dad and Uncle Ray and their sisters decided to throw a big shindig. It's turning into a regular family reunion with most of the kinfolks coming into town."

Andi could live with the disappointment of not seeing him. She had a harder time handling the fact that he didn't want her to go. Years of masking her feelings in public helped her to keep the hurt out of her voice. "I'm sure you'll have a wonderful time. I hope they have a big cake."

He chuckled. "They will and a ton of other food. I'll give you a call when I get back."

"Sure. Have a nice time." Andi spent the next few minutes rationalizing why he didn't ask her to go. The reasons varied from having limited accommodations to the fact that her presence might very well take the limelight away from his grandfather, which she would loathe.

She could make all kinds of excuses, but in her heart, she knew the main reason he didn't invite her—taking her to such an important family gathering would be like announcing over a loud speaker that their relationship was serious.

Fifteen

❧

Wade stood on the dark back porch of his aunt's farm house, looking out across the bare field that would soon be green with cotton plants. Even in the moonlight, it seemed as if he could see along the smooth, flat plains clear to Nebraska. The clock on the mantle struck ten-thirty, and he heard the creak of the screen door. He turned, smiling at his grandfather as he walked out. "I thought you were going to bed."

"I am directly, but I need a minute to unwind after all the doin's today."

"It was some party, but I'm glad we came on out here and left all the others behind."

His grandfather laughed. "Those daughters of mine will still be gossiping come sunup. It was a real treat to see all the family together." The old gentleman eased into the rocking chair on the porch and sighed contentedly. "So, tell me about the woman that's got you out here howlin' at the moon."

"I was just thinking."

"Noisy thinkin' with all that heavy sighing. Has to be a woman involved."

"You're right." Wade hesitated. "I'm in love, and I don't know what to do about it."

"A man usually asks the woman he loves to marry him. Unless she's already married. Then you've got a real problem."

"She's not married, but she might as well be."

"Career woman?" At Wade's nod, he continued, "Funny thing about love, son, it hits when you least expect it, and usually without regard for what the other person does for a living. Of course, you've probably already figured that out. I reckon what you're worried about is if her career will be more important than her husband and kids, if you have any."

"That's part of it." Wade reluctantly looked up at his grandfather. "A big part of it. Do you follow country music much these days?"

"Some. I may be old but I ain't deaf. I like a good tune as much as I ever did, although they don't play the old timers on the radio much anymore. Mostly I watch the Grand Ol' Opry. You in love with a musician?"

"Yes, sir. Her name is Andi Carson."

"Shoot, son. Half the men in West Texas are in love with that little gal. Saw her on the Opry three or four months back. I would have watched it anyway, but Ray called to make sure I knew a Buckley gal was goin' to be on the show. I saw her on one of those country talk shows a few days later, too. She's a pretty little thing and can sing like a nightingale if I remember right."

"You remember right. She's been back in Buckley for several weeks, recovering from pneumonia, and we've been seeing a lot of each other." Wade rested his head against the post and closed his eyes. "I love her with all my heart and have for a long time. I think she loves me, too, but I can't see how it could ever work.

She was on the road for two hundred days last year. She says she's cutting down on touring, but I couldn't stand it if she was gone half that time. And I can't ask her to quit. She's a star and has worked hard to get there. It wouldn't be right to take all that away from her."

"And if you did ask, and she quit, you'd always be afraid that she would regret it and blame you. You're afraid she will grow to hate you and your children and leave, like your mother did. That's the heart of it, isn't it son?"

"Yes, sir. I don't like to admit I'm a coward, but I guess I am."

"I wouldn't call that being a coward. I reckon she's a real hard worker and a determined little gal to get to where she is. Talent alone wouldn't have done it. So tell me about her. Does she change her opinions and beliefs to suit the situation? Is fame more important to her than anything else? Does she have a quick, mean temper? Does the world have to revolve around her and only her? Do you always have to question what she says, wondering if it's the truth or a lie?"

Wade straightened. His grandfather may have been pretending to ask about Andi, but he was talking about Wade's mother, and in doing so, clearly pointed out some of the major differences between the two women.

"Is she like your mother, Wade?"

"No, sir. She's an angel. She's honest, loving and caring, and stands firm in her beliefs. She's passionate sometimes about her opinions, but she doesn't have a hot temper. I don't know how important money and fame are, but she did say making music was as important to her as breathing."

"Then her career is the main problem, not whether you can trust her with your heart."

185

"I don't know, Grandpa. When couples are apart too much, they get lonely. There's an awful lot of temptation out there, especially on the road like that." Wade sighed heavily and noticed a tiny smile flit across his grandfather's face. "Guess you were right about the noise." He smiled ruefully, then grew somber. "I can't ask her to quit. It's too important to her, too many people love her and her music. It wouldn't be fair."

"If a person is prone to temptation, it has a way of findin' you no matter where you are. As for her career, reach some kind of compromise. Being with her part of the time has to be better than **not** being with her at all."

"I don't know. Sometimes, I think it would be better to end it, to say goodbye once and try to get over her. My heart will break every time she goes away."

"It'll hurt all right, but sometimes being apart shows you how good it is when you're together. I guess what it comes down to is whether or not her love is the lasting kind, and that's something only the Lord knows for sure. Even the greatest love can be destroyed under the right circumstances, so frettin' about it isn't going to do you a bit of good. Will she be leaving soon?"

"Yes, sir. I expect in a week or two."

"Then why are you sittin' here talking to me?"

Wade laughed. "Because it's your birthday and because I don't know many old codgers who are as much fun to talk to."

"Well, I'm through talkin'." Mr. Jamison stood and turned toward the door. "Head on home at first light, boy. Make hay while the sun shines."

Wade followed his grandfather inside. "You sure you don't mind?"

"If I'd minded, boy, I wouldn't have suggested it. I'm gonna have more grandkids and great-grandkids out here tomorrow than I'll know what to do with. Don't need you around takin' up space, too." The older man winked. "I'll expect you to bring her up to see me first chance you get."

"Yes, sir, I will." Wade hugged him. "I love you, Grandpa."

"Love you, too, son. You're my favorite grandchild."

"I heard you say exactly the same thing to Sissy this afternoon." Wade draped his arm over the old man's shoulders as they walked toward his bedroom.

"Meant it, too. Whichever one I'm talking to is my favorite at that minute. All twenty-three of them."

Wade didn't get away as quickly as he had hoped, but he still slipped into the church pew beside Andi before the congregation finished the first hymn. When she looked up, her face glowing at the sight of him, it was almost more than he could do to keep from pulling her into his arms. When the song ended and every one turned to greet their neighbors, he could see only Andi.

"I thought you weren't coming home until later."

"I got lonesome."

"I'm glad you're here."

As everyone sat down, he caught her hand, holding it tight. He leaned close to her ear. "Right now, I wish we were down on the creek without another soul in sight." She turned slightly pink and squeezed his hand, letting him know she wished it, too.

Guests were introduced, and the pastor made a few announcements, then smiled broadly. "As you probably saw in the bulletin, we have a baby dedication this morning." He asked a young couple to bring their baby down to the front, a little boy about six months old.

"Isn't he cute," whispered Andi. "Look at those little coveralls." She shifted closer to Wade so she could see the little guy better. "And those tiny tennis shoes. Oh, what a sweetie."

Wade watched her face as she smiled and sighed softly. He barely heard Clint ask the parents if they promised to nurture the boy in God's love and to teach him about Jesus. When the minister asked the church members to promise to pray for him and offer support and guidance whenever they could, he murmured his affirmative reply along with the rest of them, but he never looked away from her beautiful face, from the glistening mist in her eyes.

Pastor said something, then a loud "huhhh" sounded over the microphone. As Andi and the rest of the congregation laughed, Wade looked back toward the front of the church. The minister now held the baby, and the kid had a firm grip on the microphone and was trying to eat it.

"Is anyone going to be electrocuted here?" asked Clint with a grin, looking at the man who ran the sound system. The man shook his head, and the minister relaxed. The baby kept chewing on the microphone, grinning every time he made a noise. "I think we may have another famous singer in our midst someday," said Clint. He cradled the little boy on one arm, letting him continue to hold onto the microphone. "Andrew, may the Lord bless you and keep you, may he make his face to shine upon you—"

He was interrupted by another "huhhh," and a squeal of delight.

Andi laughed, looking up at Wade with joy shining in her

eyes. He couldn't resist putting his arm around her shoulders.

"And give you peace, now and forever more." The minister eased the microphone away from Andrew and handed it to his mother, holding him close so he could pray. The little boy's face began to pucker, and Clint talked fast. "Lord, we thank you for little Andrew. We ask you to be close to him all his days, shower him with your love, and keep him from harm. Amen."

Clint handed the baby back to his mother and the little boy choked back a sob. As they walked to their seats, Andrew cast a longing look at the microphone, evoking more laughter.

"He must be teething," whispered Andi.

"Or practicing to become a public speaker," Wade murmured as they stood to sing another song.

He didn't hear much of the sermon. Too many hopes and dreams got in the way of his concentration. Andi held his hand and fidgeted for the remainder of the service, so he figured she didn't get too much out of the message, either. The instant the benediction ended, he asked, "May I take you home?"

She nodded, and they drifted toward the door, politely avoiding lengthy conversations with those who greeted them.

Dawn intercepted them near the Chevy coupe. "I have to stop by the grocery store for some milk." She winked at Wade. "Maybe I'll do a scientific study of the ingredients in all the different cereals while I'm there."

"You do that."

It took them less than five minutes to get to Dawn's house. Once they were inside, he pushed the door closed with his foot and pulled her into his arms, kissing her deeply. Holding her close, he buried his face in her hair. "You smell good."

"I ought to. This stuff costs a fortune." She kissed his throat. "You smell good, too."

"Drug store special. Whatever was on sale."

"So frugal." She looked up at him. "Thanks for coming home early."

"Grandpa booted me out. Said he was tired of all my lonesome sighs."

"So you did miss me."

"Yes, ma'am." He leaned against the front door and settled her comfortably in his embrace.

"Well?" she asked, her voice muffled against his chest.

"Well, what?"

"How much did you miss me?"

More than I thought possible. More than I dare admit. "Oh, a thimbleful."

"What?!" She pushed against his chest, but he only eased his hold, not letting her go completely. She glared at him. "You can do better than that, Wade Jamison."

He shook his head. "No, a thimbleful is the best I can do. 'Course it belonged to the Jolly Green Giant or more likely, Mrs. Giant. It was real purty, all covered with rubies and pearls. He said it had been handed down from her grandmother or great-aunt or somebody. Had been a present from the giant king because she was such a beautiful—"

"Wade?"

"Yes, darlin'?"

"Shut up and kiss me."

"Yes, ma'am."

$\mathcal{S}ixteen$

By noon on Wednesday, the line of people waiting for Andi's autograph signing circled the block. The sheriff and police chief decided to close off the block of Main Street in front of Dawn's store, Memory Lane, to ease the flow of people and lessen the possibility of someone being hit by a car.

Being Andi's first public appearance since her illness, Kyle arranged for a brief press conference before the autographing. Reporters from the local newspapers were invited, as well as people from the Dallas and Nashville papers, the country music fan magazines, and The Nashville Network. Andi talked with them inside Dawn's store and posed for pictures as Wade watched her, his back to the front door. The first several questions were about her illness, pumping for details of her hospital stay.

"Are you still having any health problems, Miss Carson?"

She grinned at the young reporter from Sidell. "Do I look sick?"

He blushed and grinned back. "No, ma'am. You look fantastic."

"Thank you." She winked at him. "Your name is now on my list of preferred interviewers." The young man and the other reporters laughed. She glanced at Wade. He shook his head with a smile, and she looked back at the media people. "I'm feeling wonderful and have plenty of energy. According to my doctor I'm fit as a fiddle. Of course, I never have figured out how to tell if a fiddle is fit or not...." Performer that she was, Andi waited a few beats while her audience chuckled. "There is a bit of scarring in my lungs from the pneumonia, but it doesn't hamper my singing, and thankfully, my vocal cords weren't damaged from all the coughing."

"Are you anxious to get back to work? And will you be rescheduling the concerts you missed?"

"We are rescheduling as many as we can. My manager, Kyle Wilson, is working things out. You know how it is, the singer is the last to know where she's going, so I can't give you the details. Kyle will be releasing the information as soon as the dates are finalized."

She couldn't keep from glancing at Wade. He was making a great effort to keep his expression unconcerned, but she saw the turmoil in his eyes. "I'm looking forward to going back to work in some ways, mainly to fulfill my commitment to my fans. They've been so wonderful throughout this time. I can't begin to count the number of letters and gifts I've received. It's been over-whelming. And, of course, I love singing. But it has also been very good to rest and have some peace and quiet. My time here has been very special, and I'm not anxious for it to end."

"Do you think you might be moving back to Buckley?" asked the editor from the local paper.

"I'm thinking about it."

"Miss Carson, we heard you were at the mall in Sidell recently with a very handsome cowboy," said the female reporter from one of the fan magazines.

"That's true."

The reporter followed Andi's gaze as she smiled at Wade. "We also heard that he almost got in a fight with three men who insisted on an autograph even though you were ready to leave."

"The key word here is *almost*. He convinced the men that I was tired and needed to leave, using words not fists."

"But would he have fought them?"

Andi smiled. "Most Texas men will fight if necessary to protect their women."

The woman looked slyly at Wade, then back at Andi, her eyes sparkling. "And are you his woman, Miss Carson?"

Oops. "Sneaky little thing, aren't you?" she said with a smile. "I was just using a figure of speech." *More like a slip of the tongue.* "Wade is an old friend from high school. He is also a terrific bodyguard. Now, folks, I need to move on outside and get an early start on the autographing. We're liable to be here until dark as it is. There are some refreshments next door, please help yourself. Thank you so much for coming."

Wade opened the door and the reporters filed past, each one giving him an assessing glance. As the woman from the fan magazine strolled by, she winked and smiled coyly. He smiled politely and shut the door behind her, giving Andi a few minutes breather time before she faced the crowd.

"I'm sorry. I'm afraid you may find your name in a magazine in the near future."

"As long as she puts in the 'very handsome cowboy' part, I

won't complain." His gaze caressed her face, sending her pulse racing. "It was bound to happen sooner or later. I don't mind having my name linked to yours, unless they make up some outlandish gossip and try to hurt you."

Her heart did a triple somersault, and she warned herself not to read too much into what he said. "Those folks won't. They're not like the tabloids or some of the Hollywood magazines. They may speculate a little but not in a way meant to hurt. Well, I guess I'd better go greet the 'screaming hordes', as Dawn calls them."

"They look fairly tame." He slipped his arm around her waist, detaining her with the slight pressure of his hand. "By the way, you answered one question wrong."

She looked up, meeting his warm gaze. "Which one?"

"The one about you being my woman."

This time, she knew he could hear her heart pounding for certain, but before she could say anything, he winked and opened the front door.

"Your loyal subjects await, my lady," he drawled, gently propelling her through the doorway.

The day was sunny but not hot, so Andi sat at a table outside in front of Dawn's store, with a prominent sign strategically placed behind her giving the date of Memory Lane's grand opening. Wade sat on a high stool to the left in back of her. Two deputy sheriffs flanked them, spaced about fifteen feet on either side of her table. The sheriff wandered though the crowd, watching for potential problems, while kissing babies and gathering votes for the next election.

Rosemary and Harold, along with a couple of other people Dawn had recruited for the museum board, presided over the free cookies and soda Andi had provided. The refreshments were served inside the old Knox's Department Store building, which Mr. Knox's heirs had donated to the city. A big banner, made by the high school cheerleaders, hung across one of the front display windows, announcing it as the future sight of the museum. Dawn sat at another table, handling ticket sales for the dance on Friday night and taking donations for the museum.

Andi put her signature on everything from pieces of paper and autograph books to magazine articles to T-shirts. She even signed one young man's guitar. Often during the afternoon, she noticed media people at work—reporters interviewing the fans, photographers taking pictures of her and the crowd, and two video camera crews, one from the television station in Sidell and one from The Nashville Network.

She had been signing autographs, visiting a minute with each fan, and posing with them for photographs for almost four hours, when Wade slid off his stool and stepped up beside her. She could tell something was wrong by his tense stance. She looked up at the next person in line and immediately recognized the cowboy who had almost gotten into a fight with Wade at the mall.

"Thank you so much for coming over," she said, smiling sweetly, hoping to avoid another scene. "I'm sorry I had to leave the other day."

A flush spread across the young man's face. "That's all right, ma'am. You were doin' folks a favor as it was." He handed her a stuffed dog with floppy ears, wearing a white fringed vest. "I'd appreciate it if you could sign on the vest for Lacey. That's my girl, but she had to be out of town." He placed a country music magazine on the table, open to the list of top forty country hits. Her last single was number one on the chart. "And this is for me, Billy Bob."

"I'd be happy to. Where are your friends?" she asked as she quickly inscribed the vest.

"They had to work. I didn't tell them I was comin' over. I was afraid they'd call in sick or something and come, too. I wanted to apologize for the way we acted the other day, and I was afraid I'd chicken out if they were here. I am sorry, ma'am."

"That's sweet of you, Billy Bob." She handed him the signed magazine. "And I think you'd have been man enough to apologize even if your friends were here."

He smiled, thanked her, and moved out of the way, nodding respectfully at Wade as he did so.

Wade leaned over, murmuring in her ear, "You're the one who's sweet." He drew back slightly, relishing her sweet smile and the pleasure in her eyes when she looked at him. "Want something else to drink?"

"Please. A Dr. Pepper would be great."

"Coming right up."

She had writer's cramp by the time she finished near six o'clock, but this time, no one was turned away. They went back to Dawn's, accompanied by everyone on the museum board and ordered several large pizzas from a restaurant near the interstate.

Wade rubbed her right hand while she fed him a bite of super-deluxe pizza with her left. "Did you sell some tickets?" she asked Dawn.

"Thirty," mumbled Dawn around a bite of pepperoni and black olive pizza. She chewed, swallowed, and smiled. "And collected fifty dollars in donations. We're raking in a bundle on the dance, since almost everybody is donating their time. We're paying the band since they're college students and need the money. It shouldn't be a problem; we've sold over five hundred tickets. It's a good thing it's a street dance. We'd never find a place in Buckley big enough, although the city council did say we could use the new museum sight if it rained. We'd still be way too crowded."

Rosemary and Harold stayed after the other board members left and joined them in several games of dominoes. Claiming that her hands were too tired to hold anything, Andi teamed up with Wade and had great fun arguing with him about which pieces to play. After the other couple left, she walked out to the car with him. "Did your friend Grant come today? I know he wasn't playing bodyguard, but I saw too many people to remember their names."

"No, I didn't call him about it since we didn't need him. I was afraid it might make his knee hurt if he had to stand for very long. It was bothering him last week when he was at the house. He may come to the dance, though. I sent him a ticket."

"Playing matchmaker?"

"Maybe. Dawn would be good for him. Mostly, I thought it would do him good to get out. All he does is work and go visit his daughter every Sunday. He's goin' to turn plumb anti-social if he doesn't start being around people." He smiled. "Come to think of it, he never was real social, at least not in the polished sense of the word."

"And you want to set this man up with our sweet little Dawn?"

"Put a little spice in her life," he said with a wicked grin.

"I'm not sure she's ready for jalapenos."

He threw back his head and laughed. "She's sweet and sassy enough to mellow him out." His expression sobered. "Don't tell her he might come to the dance. I wouldn't want her to be disappointed."

"She's going to be so busy between now and then that it probably wouldn't make much difference to her anyway, but I won't say anything."

The wind blew Andi's hair across her face. Wade gently pushed it aside with one hand. "I was proud of you today. You had something nice to say to every one of those people, and your smile never wavered. You made each one feel special."

"They are."

"So are you." He lowered his head, kissing her tenderly. "Good night, sweetheart."

"Good night, precious man."

"I like the sound of that." Wade eased away, getting into the red coupe. "I'll see you Friday about six."

"I'll be ready. Wear something comfortable. Your boots will be smokin' by the end of the party."

"I don't know if I ever told you, but I don't do line dances."

"Can you put one foot in front of the other and go slowly around the room without tripping your partner?"

"I can, and I'm real good at hanging onto her."

"That's all I need. See you Friday."

Articles about the autographing showed up in the papers on Thursday, each accompanied by various photographs of Andi signing autographs for her fans or chatting with them. The Sidell television station ran a feature on her and the event during both their noon and evening news programs.

Wade stretched out in his recliner that evening and flipped on the "Country News" program. As usual, he set the video recorder to tape the show in case they had something on about Andi.

After the broadcaster greeted the viewers, she launched right into a segment about Andi. "We're happy to report that singer Andrea Carson has recovered from the pneumonia that sent her to the hospital several weeks ago and postponed the rest of her tour. Andi came out of seclusion in a big way yesterday afternoon, signing autographs for a huge crowd for almost six hours in her home town of Buckley, Texas."

The scene switched to film of Andi laughing with one of her fans and signing the hem of his T-shirt. "Andi told our 'Country News' reporter that she's feeling wonderful and will soon resume her tour, making up as many of the canceled shows as can be rescheduled. She said the autograph signing was a way of thanking her friends and neighbors in Buckley for protecting her privacy and giving her the peace and quiet she needed to rest and recover."

The camera panned the crowd, showing a portion of the hundreds of people who were there. "Andi will also be singing a few songs Friday night at a benefit dance in Buckley to help raise money for a new historical museum in the town."

The camera moved back to Andi, and Wade catapulted out of the chair. He was in the picture, too, standing by her side like a Texas Ranger ready to single-handedly take on a band of desperadoes. Billy Bob stood in front of her, smiling as she handed him the signed magazine.

When the young man moved aside, Wade smiled and leaned close to Andi, whispering something in her ear. He moved back slightly, his countenance revealing more than a hint of how he felt about her. They talked briefly, then he straightened and turned away. She watched him leave, smiling the way any man would want his woman to smile at him—full of sugar and spice and everything nice.

The woman news anchor smiled and lifted one perfectly arched brow. "Hmmm. Looks like Andi may have found something even better than peace and quiet in her home town. According to the folks we talked to, the handsome man hovering protectively around her is Wade Jamison, an old high school friend and local rancher."

Wade hit the mute button and sank back down to the chair, momentarily stunned. Quick, hot anger surged through him at the invasion of their privacy, but he quickly snuffed it out. He had been in a very public place with a famous entertainer. It came with the territory. He rewound the tape and hit the play button as the telephone rang. Muting the sound, he stared at the television and picked up the phone.

"Well, boy, looks to me like you cut the hay and already started baling it."

Wade laughed, watching the scene again. "Hi, Grandpa. Kinda made a spectacle of myself, didn't I?"

"True, honest feelings never hurt anybody. There's many a man who would give everything he has for that little gal to look at him like that. She loves you, son. Don't you ever doubt it."

Wade stopped the video, freezing the frame of her face as she gazed at him. He took a deep breath and slowly released it. "You may be right."

"Of course I'm right. Always am." The older man's tone turned serious. "This is just a taste of what you're in for, son. If you can't live with it, now's the time to say so before you get in any deeper. Now, hang up the phone and call your lady. She's probably worried sick about what you're thinking."

"I don't know what I'm thinking, Grandpa."

"Well, figure it out fast."

The line went dead and Wade hung up the receiver. Looking back over the past weeks, he realized he hadn't been much good at keeping his feelings for Andi hidden, because in his heart, he didn't want to. "She's mine. And I don't care who knows it. I want every man out there who wants her for himself to know she belongs to me. Only me."

He reached for the telephone with a hand that trembled slightly. When he said the words to her for the first time, it would be in person, but he didn't want her to worry. He knew that after his behavior of the past week, she'd be concerned.

Dawn answered, then turned the phone over to Andi. He heard uncertainty in her hello.

"Hello, darlin'." He spoke quietly in the same gentle tone he would use with a frightened horse, but added an extra measure of warmth. "Well, I reckon now I know how it feels to be on national television."

"Wade, I'm sorry. I should never have asked you to come to the—"

"Hush, sweetheart," he said tenderly, his voice deep and rough with emotion. "Don't apologize for makin' me the proudest man in all of Texas."

Seventeen

W histling, Wade tucked his wallet into his pocket and picked up the keys to the Chevy coupe from the dresser, preparing to leave for the dance.

He had plans for the evening, ones that involved baring his heart and soul. He would take Andi home before the end of the dance and entice her out to the back porch to look at the full moon. Somewhere along the way, he'd tell her he loved her, couldn't live without her, and ask her to marry him. It sounded so easy, but he knew it wouldn't be.

What if she says no? What if she's only interested in me because I'm here, nice and handy? Wade looked in the mirror, frowning at the doubt he saw in his eyes and the fear he felt in his heart. "She will say yes," he said forcefully, trying to vanquish the uncertainty.

He put his hands on the edge of the dresser and hung his head, staring at the jumble of ballpoint pens, pile of pennies, and a couple of small screws that had wound up there. "Maybe you've got a few screws loose yourself, Jamison, for even thinkin' she might want to spend her life with you."

He took a deep breath and straightened, taking a handkerchief from the top drawer and stuffing it into the back pocket of his jeans. "Lord, am I seeing love in her eyes because I want it so desperately? Please give me wisdom. And if I ask her to marry me and she refuses, help me have the grace to accept it."

The police roped off all three blocks of downtown Main Street for the benefit dance. The stage was a flatbed trailer parked in the intersection of Chestnut and Main. The museum committee had men posted at every corner of the roped off area, taking and selling tickets and stamping the hands of those who paid, so they could come and go at will.

Folding chairs borrowed from a couple of churches lined the sidewalks near the buildings. More chairs were set up in the museum, along with a refreshment center run by the newly formed Friends of Buckley Museum. Wade thought half the women in town and the surrounding area had baked cookies to be sold for a quarter apiece. Dawn had talked the local soft drink distributors into donating cases of pop for them to sell. A large supply of paper cups sat by the water fountain inside the building. There were no alcoholic beverages, and all the advertisements for the benefit had asked people not to bring any since this was a family outing and all ages were invited.

At exactly seven o'clock, Dawn scampered up the steps to the stage and took the microphone, handling the welcome and announcements like a pro.

Wade was pleased that Andi wore the vest he had given her. It looked particularly nice with her red blouse and light-weight denim skirt. "Have I told you how pretty you look tonight?"

"Only a couple of times," she said with a teasing smile. "But you can always tell me again. It must have something to do with the vest."

"It does look nice on you. I'm glad you like it." They moved expertly across the street, waltzing in a smooth, easy rhythm to the music. "But, sugar, you'd be beautiful wearin' a feed sack."

"And scandalous." She laughed, revealing her dimples. "I like your shirt," she said, running her finger across the pattern woven into the lustrous, emerald green material. "It's a nice color for you, brings out the green in your eyes."

"Thank you, ma'am," he drawled, pressing his hand against her back and guiding her forward as he moved backward to avoid colliding with another couple.

"Say, cowboy, I think you lied to me."

"Never, darlin'."

"Well, you stretched the truth by giving me the impression you weren't a good dancer."

"I never said I couldn't dance." He led her into a gliding turn, making her laugh. "I said I didn't do any line dances."

"Why not?"

He shrugged. "I don't know. Just seems like a real cowboy wouldn't do that sort of thing. All that hopping around and kickin' and wigglin' your feet every which way. I do enough of that dodgin' cows."

"I'm sure some real cowboys line dance, but I like you just the way you are."

At first, he worried about having his time with Andi interrupted by fans, but he soon saw that though many recognized her as they danced, they merely smiled and left them alone. He didn't know whether it was because they had seen the TNN "Country News" segment, or they simply realized she was on a date like everyone else, but he didn't care.

The song ended, but Wade and Andi remained on the dance floor, stepping lively to the next tune, a fast tempo Western swing. They started out side by side, then she crossed in front of him, and they shifted the position of their hands. He twirled her around, pulled her close, then spun her out again. He drew her back beside him, and they moved several steps forward before repeating the earlier spins.

"I told you your boots would be smokin'," she said, with a bright smile.

"Just scorched. The night is young."

"And I can tell I haven't been exercising as much as usual."

"Do you need to stop?" he asked, instantly concerned. He kept moving forward instead of spinning her.

"I'm all right. I'm having too much fun to stop."

The band, The Rustlers, was quite good, and the five young men were enjoying themselves. The lead singer ended the song with a rousing "Yee-ha!" then announced that the next one would be slow. "Now that we've got your blood pumping, we'll let you rest a bit. This is dedicated to all of you who are in love. And maybe a few who wish they were."

"Do you need to sit down?" Wade put his arm around her.

Andi looked straight into his eyes and put her hand on his shoulder. "I wouldn't miss this dance for anything."

As he held her in his arms and began to move in a slow Texas Shuffle, the crowd faded away. They existed in a world made for them alone. She rested her temple against his jaw, her contented sigh warming the side of his neck, and love welled up in his heart. The song ended far too soon.

"I'd better find something to drink. I'm supposed to sing after the next two songs."

Wade rested his hand at the small of her back as they wove their way across the crowded street to the museum. She stayed by his side as he bought two cans of root beer. "Want a cookie?"

"Not now. But I'll be dying for a brownie later." She winked at Harold, who was handling the cookie sales at the moment. He smiled and set a brownie aside for her. "Better make that two, or Wade will eat most of it." He laughed and did as she asked.

They found a couple of chairs near the window. "How did your practice with the band go this afternoon?" Wade took a long drink of the cold root beer.

"Good. They know all my songs, so it was easy to pick some." She drank some of the pop and watched the crowd.

"Think we'd better make our way over toward the stage?"

"Yes." She took a deep breath, releasing it slowly.

"What's wrong?"

"Pre-show jitters. Nervous excitement. I always get it right before I go on."

They started toward the stage. "I'm surprised you still get nervous. I'd think it would be routine by now."

"Each audience is different, and somehow, each performance is different." As they neared the steps to the stage, she grabbed hold of his hand.

"Hey, your hand is ice cold." He clasped it firmly with his own and stopped walking. When she halted, he searched her face. "You really *are* nervous."

"More than normal. I haven't done this in a while. Not since I was sick. What if my voice cracks or I forget the words or hit a wrong note?"

He put his arms around her and held her gently. "Nothing bad is going to happen. And even if it does, folks will understand. Everybody here loves you, Andi. They're thrilled with the chance to hear you sing, and it won't matter a bit if you're a little rusty." The song ended, and he looked up, meeting the lead singer's gaze. Wade nodded, then gave her a little squeeze, plucked the soft drink can from her hand, and escorted her to within a few feet of the steps. "Send them to the moon, sweetheart."

Dawn ran up and gave her a hug. "Thanks, cuz. You're the greatest."

"Get out front, you two, or you'll miss the show." Andi smiled at them, took a deep breath, and moved to the bottom step, resting her hand on the rail.

Wade and Dawn worked their way through the group of dancers waiting for the next song until they were far enough back for a good view but still close enough for Wade to quickly return to the stage steps when Andi was through.

Someone spotted Andi standing at the bottom of the steps and word spread like wildfire. The crowd surged forward, dancing forgotten. Standing beside Wade, Dawn was jostled by the excited fans. He put his hand on her arm to draw her over in front of him, but stopped when Grant Adams moved in behind her. When she looked at Wade, he smiled and released her arm, shifting his gaze to Grant and tipping his head slightly.

Dawn glanced over her shoulder, and Grant lowered his head, speaking directly into her ear to be heard over of the noise.

"Ma'am, if you could scoot up a step, Wade and I can block you from the crowd. A little thing like you could get squished and nobody would know it."

Dawn did as he suggested, and he followed so that he stood even with Wade and behind her. She looked back to thank him, but the band leader addressed the audience over the microphone, making it impossible to be heard. So she smiled and mouthed "thank you," and was rewarded with a hint of a smile in return. Turning her gaze to the stage, a little thrill shivered through her. A cleaned up Grant Adams was even better than the hard-working man, although he still made her think of an outlaw.

"Folks, we're glad you're enjoying our music, but we're smart enough to know you didn't come to see The Rustlers. Your wait is over." He turned toward the steps and held out his arm. "Ladies and gentlemen, Buckley's pride and the lady you all came to see and hear—Andi Carson!"

The crowd went crazy, screaming, whistling, and clapping. The noise level increased as Andi ran up the steps and onto the stage, a brilliant smile on her face. The lead singer handed her a microphone, and she greeted the audience. "Are y'all having a good time?"

The nearby windows rattled from the roaring response.

"I'm having fun, too, dancing to The Rustlers' music. Aren't they great?"

Another roar of approval.

"I want to thank you for supporting our new museum and for coming out tonight. I hope you get your money's worth."

"Just seein' you standin' there healthy is worth every penny and then some!" a man called from the audience. Everyone clapped and whistled. Wade heard more than one hearty "amen."

Andi blinked back tears and hung her head for a few seconds. She moved the microphone away and cleared her throat, smiling at the crowd, and they quieted down. "Thank you." She had to clear her throat again. "Thank you for all the good wishes and especially for your prayers. Without those prayers and God's loving grace, I wouldn't be here today." She took a deep breath and grinned mischievously. "Now, before I go and get all weepy, we'd better do some singin'."

She nodded to the musicians, and they started in on a rollicking number that was a combination of country and rhythm and blues. She pranced across the stage, belting out the first line, and the crowd went wild, clapping and stomping their feet in time to the music.

Wade half expected some of the old buildings to come crashing down, but he didn't look to see if they were shaking. He was mesmerized. She had transformed right before his eyes from being insecure to being in complete control of herself, the music, and the audience. She drew the spectators into the fun, teasing the men one minute, and pointing out the error of their ways the next, nodding in agreement with the women. Like a consummate actress, her facial expressions and body movements changed to fit each line of the song. Musically, she never missed a note, hitting high and low and everything in between with breathtaking power and clarity.

When he had seen her perform in Boulder, he had been amazed and enthralled, but even there, with all the fancy lights and special effects that were missing here, she had not been so vibrant, so alive. So joyful. The song ended to deafening applause and her smile became radiant.

No man can give her the adulation and sense of power that she gets from an audience.

"Whoo-ee!" Grant leaned closer so Wade could hear him. "Your woman is something else."

My woman. He clung to the thought like a lifeline.

The next song was a high speed boogie-woogie that had Andi, as well as the folks on the fringe of the crowd, dancing energetically. Then she changed the pace again on the third tune, this time to the joyful beat of Western swing.

Wade felt his dreams slipping farther away with each new song.

She paused a minute to catch her breath and picked up her guitar from a stand at the back of the stage. Slipping the strap over her head and across one shoulder, she stepped back to the microphone and grinned. "Time to slow down before I wear out."

She played the slow solo introduction to a song which Wade, and almost everyone else, recognized as her most recent hit single, a melancholy tale of love gone wrong that had reached number one on the charts. He had expected her to sing it due to its popularity but braced himself for the feelings he knew it would evoke. Her eyes drifted closed and her voice grew thick as if she were holding back tears.

He clenched his fists until they ached and looked past the stage, unable to watch her beautiful face. Was she only acting out the emotions portrayed in the song, or did she feel them in her heart? Was she merely making music to touch those who listened, or was she telling him goodbye? Somehow, he stood still when he wanted to flee, lasting the length of the song, and even clapped when it was done.

Grant looked at him, his eyes filled with concern. "It's just a song, buddy."

Dawn heard him and glanced up at Wade. When she stretched up on tip-toe to speak to him, he lowered his head. "Don't look so forlorn. She's only singing it because everyone expects her to."

He smiled, knowing she meant well, but he didn't believe her.

Andi looked back at the band. "Looks like we've got every-body wallowing in sorrow." The band all nodded in unison, wearing mournful expressions, and a ripple of laughter went through the audience. "Reckon we'd better brighten them up?" They nodded again and the drummer hit a snappy beat. The rest of the band quickly joined in, and Andi swung around toward the crowd, looking directly at Wade and flirting shamelessly.

Give me a man I can call my own,
A six foot hunk who's big and strong,
The kind of guy who likes to dance,
A sweet talkin' man who loves romance.

The song was on her first album, and she once said she had written it to be a little silly, but his spirits soared anyway. Maybe there was hope after all.

When the audience joined in on the chorus, she winked at him and looked away, moving around on stage to include every-one for the rest of the song.

"Thank you, you've been wonderful!" She waved, blew a kiss to the crowd, and started to leave, but they began to chant her name, begging for more. She looked at the band leader, and he grinned, pointing back to the middle of the stage. She shrugged, smiled, and walked back to the microphone to tremendous applause. After a few minutes, she held up her hands to quiet them. "Thank you." She smiled sweetly. "How can I resist when you ask so nicely?"

"I'd like to share a new song with you, one I wrote recently," she said, absently strumming chords. "When I was a little girl, my great-grandmother told me how my great-grandfather, who was a cowboy, spent months trying to capture a beautiful wild mustang. This is Great-grandpa Buck's story, and I have a feeling it is only one of many I'll be telling over the years, even though I never knew him.

"I'd like to dedicate it to each cowboy here tonight, for your indomitable spirit, your love of the land, and your quest to be free." Her gaze locked with Wade's. "And your tender heart."

It was a stirring ballad, sung with exquisite perception and passion, a tale of determination and valor of both man and beast, of desperate flight and relentless pursuit, of imminent capture and last minute mercy from a man who understood the need to run free.

Wade thought it was the most beautiful thing she had ever done. All around him, people wiped their eyes. Even Grant swallowed hard and cleared his throat. Dawn cried openly, ruining her makeup, and gratefully accepted Grant's handkerchief without apology.

Andi wiped her cheeks and took a minute to collect her composure. "I've gotten reacquainted with an old friend these past few weeks. Because of him, I'm alive today. Because of him, I'll live in heaven for eternity, and you can, too. He's kind and loving and full of grace and forgiveness. If you don't know him, I hope you'll seek him out. His name is Jesus." She played an intricate introduction on the guitar, and when she began to sing, the crowd listened in awed silence.

I have a friend, won't you meet him, too?
He gave his life for me and you.

Wade's eyes misted and his throat burned with unshed tears as Andi sang of the Master's love, his healing touch, and his saving grace. In singing about the Savior, her voice took on an ethereal quality, a reverence and love that would melt the hardest heart. The incredible beauty of her singing confirmed his belief that God would use her to reach souls no one else could reach. Blessed though he was by her music, his dream of a life with her withered and all but died.

How could he ask Andi to stay with him when God had far greater plans for her?

Eighteen

༄

Shortly after her performance, Andi asked Wade to take her home. Although she had greatly enjoyed both dancing with him and singing, she felt emotionally drained. Singing about her great-grandfather had affected her more deeply than she had thought it would. Not only had it renewed the long-held wish that she could have known him, it spoke of a time lost and a freedom for which many yearned, including the man she loved.

Taking the step to share about Jesus had drawn upon her courage and jumbled her nerves. Once she got into the song, her fears had evaporated. God filled her with such peace that she knew she had done the right thing and with such joy that her heart had overflowed. She also knew she had never sung better.

Wade had complimented her on her performance, especially the last two songs, and told her how pleased he was that she talked about Jesus. Otherwise, he had been silent on the short trip back to the house. She supposed it was because he knew she would be leaving soon. Tonight proved that she was physically fit. A week, maybe two was the longest she could hope for until she had to say goodbye.

She watched him through the windshield as he came around the Blazer to open her door. *Surely, he knows it doesn't have to be forever.* She had done everything except come right out and say it, and she couldn't bring herself to go any farther. After the way he had acted during the week and earlier in the evening, she had expected him to declare his love and ask her to marry him when he took her home. Now, he was so quiet, she wasn't so sure that would happen. He had such a problem with his mother, maybe he hadn't reached the point where he could make a lifetime commitment. It was something he had to do; she couldn't back him into a corner.

As they walked to the porch, she looped her arm through his. "Was that Grant standing with you and Dawn while I was singing?"

He nodded and smiled. "She was being bumped around by the crowd, but before I could ease her over in front of me, he showed up, moving in behind her. Made a pretty good wall, too."

"How sweet. Did they talk much? I noticed she was working in the refreshment center when we left, and I didn't see him anywhere."

"I don't think they had a chance to say more than a few words to each other." He opened the screen and took the key from her hand, unlocking the door. "The music was so loud up front that it was practically impossible to hear what anybody said." He opened the door and followed her inside. "When you were done singing, I saw her glance at her watch and look upset. She was saying something to him when I left to meet you. I think maybe she had to go straight to the concession stand for her shift."

"She mentioned this afternoon that she was working there

the last two hours. What a shame." Andi turned on a lamp, leaving the setting on low, walked over to the couch, and sat down. Pulling off her boots, she propped her feet up on the coffee table and wiggled her toes. "Ah, that feels better." Wade sat down, but not as close as she would have liked. She scooted over next to him and batted her eyelashes at him. "Hi there, big boy."

"Hello." A smile warmed his eyes as he put his arm around her shoulders.

"I enjoyed dancing with you tonight. You do mighty fine for a country fella."

"I don't spend all my time at the ranch."

"Now I'm jealous."

"There's no reason to be."

She looked up at him, inviting his kiss. He hesitated and alarm spiraled through her. She could feel him withdrawing, putting up an invisible wall between them. "Wade?"

He searched her eyes, then lowered his head quickly, kissing her with barely restrained passion. The world faded away, with all its worries and pressures. As she returned his kiss with all her love, nothing existed but him—until the loud ringing of the telephone shattered the moment.

She tensed and Wade reluctantly drew back. She took a deep breath. "I'm sorry, but I need to answer it. My folks are supposed to call tonight or tomorrow and tell me where they are going next." When he handed her the phone, she smiled regretfully.

"Hello? Oh, hi, Kyle."

"How did it go tonight?"

"Great. Didn't miss a note." She looked at Wade, disheartened by the sadness in his eyes as he moved his arm and sat back against the corner of the couch. "I sang a couple of new songs I wrote last week and the crowd loved them."

"Maybe we can put them on the next album. You sound distracted. Is Wade there?"

"Yes. So make it quick."

He laughed. "Gotcha. I managed to reschedule four more of the concerts, including the one in Tucson. That gives us twelve of the fourteen we missed."

"Wonderful." Smiling happily, she put her hand over the mouthpiece and relayed the news to Wade. He gave her a weak smile. "That should help the guys' paychecks."

"The only problem is that I had to put them on the front end of the tour, so you'll have to hit the road a week from Monday."

Andi's heart sank. "So soon?"

"It gets worse, hon," he said sympathetically. "I got a call from Lorianne Crook a few minutes ago. On Monday, they'll be running a segment about tonight's concert on "Country News." They want you to be on "Music City Tonight," too. It's a great opportunity to plug the tour dates and let everyone know you're back. You can't afford to miss it. Plus you said you had some wardrobe changes to make, and you'll need to practice with the band—especially if you have new material you want to use. I'm sorry, Andi, but you'd better come back to Nashville tomorrow afternoon. I've already made reservations."

Andi's head was spinning. She couldn't leave so soon. There was too much left unsaid, too much at stake. But she had no choice. She had obligations that had to be taken care of before she could start a new life. People depending on her. She couldn't let them down again. She looked into Wade's eyes but couldn't tell what he was thinking.

"Look at it this way, hon. The sooner you hit the road, the quicker you'll get finished, and you can search out new worlds and go where you've never gone before."

She forced a laugh in spite of the doom settling over her. "You sound like you're lining up a guest spot on *Star Trek.*" She sighed. "All right. I'll fly out tomorrow." Wade appeared shocked, then the wall went up between them again. She doubted that, at this point, any amount of talking would bring it down.

"That's my girl. Nicki sends her love."

"How is she?"

"Absolutely terrific," he said softly, making Andi wonder if she was there with him. "She and her band are clicking well. She has lots of good ideas and listens to their suggestions, too. We're cutting a demo tape on Monday. I wouldn't be surprised if she has a record deal before you head out on tour. She has so much natural talent, I'm amazed every time I hear her. Reminds me of another lady I know."

"So how were the burgers?"

He laughed. "Which time? We're becoming regulars there and at the pizza place around the corner. But I've taken her to some fancy places, too. Took her to a business party last night. Man, was she a knockout. I had to stay right with her the whole time." Andi heard a giggle and knew her suspicion was right. "We found a cute little apartment today for her, and we're going furniture shopping tomorrow. Just the bare basics, she says. She doesn't want to go into debt."

"I can't believe my ears. Hamburgers and pizza. Apartment hunting and furniture shopping. And you actually sound relaxed. Kyle, are you keeping your promise?"

"Yes, though it's not easy. This is one time I'm not going to rush. It's too important."

"I'm proud of you. I'll call when I get in." She hung up the phone and looked at Wade as he rose from the sofa. "Don't go."

"You probably have a dozen things to do to get ready to leave." He sounded distant; his manner was cold.

She jumped up from the sofa. "I can do everything in the morning. All I have to do is throw stuff in a couple of suitcases."

Walking to the door, he acted as if he hadn't heard her. "Have a good trip. When do you leave on tour?"

"A week from Monday. I have to go back now to be on next Monday's 'Music City Tonight.'"

He nodded. "Good promotion."

"Wade…"

He finally looked at her, and for a heartbeat, she saw abject misery in his eyes, then it disappeared. His face could have been carved in stone. "Goodbye, darlin'. It's been fun."

She whispered his name, but the sound faded in the still air as he walked through the door. Sinking down on the sofa, she stared at the closed door and heard the roadster's engine roar to life. *It's been fun.* Was that all their time together had meant to him? Fun?

She picked up a large throw pillow and hugged it to her aching heart, weeping. "Please God, let him just be afraid. Please let him love me."

On Monday evening, Wade sat in his recliner, staring at the clock as if it were his enemy. "Music City Tonight" would be on in two minutes. Unable to stop himself, he flicked on the television and the video recorder, turning to The Nashville Network.

A cooked frozen dinner sat on the table beside him, barely touched. He rubbed his hand over his face, weary to the bone. Sleep had evaded him completely Friday night and had been virtually a stranger both Saturday and Sunday.

His leg ached where a cow had kicked him that afternoon. He knew to be on guard when trying to doctor that old lophorn, but his thoughts had been elsewhere—the same place they had been every second since Friday night. On Andi. On the hurt in her eyes as he turned away. On the ache in his heart, the pain that never lessened but stayed with him minute by minute, wearing away his very soul.

He was a coward. He'd never thought so, but now he knew better. He'd walked away from the woman he loved, hurting her deeply, and possibly destroying himself. And he was confused. Still. He was afraid he had lost her forever, and at the same time, wondering why he thought she was his to have.

He knew God was going to use her in a mighty way. That had been evident on Sunday. Wade hadn't gone to church, but Ray told him that three newcomers had talked to the pastor after the service. None of them had ever set foot inside a church before. They were there because Andi had shared about Jesus Friday night, and because her song had kindled a yearning in their hearts that they didn't understand.

Selfishly, he wanted her for himself. He didn't want to share her with anyone, not even God. And yet, he knew he couldn't hold her. Wade shook his head, wondering if he was losing his mind.

The show came on, and he stared at the screen like a zombie, watching as someone he had never heard of sang, then was interviewed by Lorianne Crook and Charlie Chase, the popular co-hosts of the program. A dog food commercial was next, and he thought about getting a puppy, maybe a cute little golden Labrador retriever like the one on the television. *A dog would follow me everywhere. He wouldn't go wandering off all over the country.*

The show returned, and Charlie gave a short introduction about Andi. Then she came on stage, singing one of her biggest hits. Wade barely heard the music, except to note that her voice was strong and true. She looked beautiful in the magenta print gauze dress she had bought when they went shopping in Sidell—the one she said she would wear when she felt free as the wind. His stomach churned and he was vaguely glad he hadn't eaten more than a few bites of the cheese enchilada dinner.

She finished the song and went over to sit by the hosts. When the camera zoomed in for a close-up, he thought she looked a little tired and was missing some of her sparkle. They chatted about her good health and the upcoming tour, then Lorianne complimented her on her appearance.

"Thank you. I bought this while I was home. I was a little tired today, still trying to get used to having to work for a living again," she said with a big smile, "so I thought it might perk me up."

"Do you go back home to Buckley often?"

"I've only been back about four other times since I came to Nashville, for quick visits with my cousin. My folks moved away not long after I left, so I didn't have as much reason to go back as I might have otherwise."

"How was it this time, since you stayed so long? I know you were probably too sick to get out much at first, but how about later?" asked Charlie. "Has it changed?"

"It has changed in many ways, but some things were like they've always been. The kids still hang out at the same hamburger joint and the old drug store is still there. But a lot of the businesses have closed. I saw some of my old friends and made some new ones. Generally, folks left me alone."

They talked a while longer, plugging the tour and the upcoming dates. Wade was both relieved and disappointed that neither his name nor any hint about him ever came up. She sang another song. Then she was gone.

He shut off the television, but set the video player to record the "Country News." Walking into the bedroom, he caught sight of his reflection in the mirror. He hadn't shaved since Friday and couldn't remember when he showered last. His shirt and jeans looked as if he had worn them for days. Maybe he had. His eyes had dark circles beneath them, and he looked as haggard and miserable as he felt.

Andi had been beautiful. She had been at ease, performed well, and seemed bright and cheerful. She was surviving, even happy, without him.

Nineteen

❧

"Just listen to that crowd! She's a hit! Didn't I tell you she was fantastic?"

The image of Wade's smiling face faded from her mind, and Andi looked at Kyle, wondering why he was practically jumping up and down. She slowly came out of the sweet, hazy daydream to reality.

"Four minutes till you're on, Andi," called her road manager. He walked over to her side. "Are you all right?"

She nodded. "Just drifting a little."

"Well, get back on course, will ya? You go on stage in three and a half minutes."

"I'm with you." *Lord, please help me not to think of Wade. I don't want to let these folks down.* To her dismay, she realized she had missed more than half of Nicki's debut performance. She had to start functioning better, or she would ruin the whole tour. She'd been inattentive during rehearsals, making them run longer than they should have. When she and Nicki had gone shopping earlier in the week, Nicki wound up picking out all Andi's new clothes because all she could think about was the day Wade had taken her shopping. She'd sat in the dressing room of one of Nashville's most expensive shops, crying her eyes out.

She took a couple of deep breaths and walked over to a microphone behind the side curtain. Nicki had finished her last solo song to tremendous applause. Kyle had been right. The crowd loved her.

It was time for their duet, and Andi's grand entrance, although the audience had no idea she was about to sing. No announcement was made, so everyone assumed Nicki was going to do another number by herself. Wade had suggested this duet, but she had never told him how she was going to use it. *I wish you were here, my love. I need you.* Heart pounding, she took the cordless microphone from the stand and focused all her attention on the others on stage.

The keyboard player led off, then Nicki came in:

Grandpa's watch lies on the mantle
Its hands forever still.

Off stage, Andi sang the next few lines, an octave higher:

But his love shines in my grandma's eyes
And it always will.

A murmur went through the crowd as people recognized Andi's pure, distinctive voice. They stretched their necks and wiggled in their seats, trying to see where she was.

Nicki sang again:

Looking back across the past
The years all fade away

Andi came in where Nicki left off:

For in her heart, she holds him still,
Just like yesterday.

Their voices blended in perfect harmony on the chorus as Andi slowly walked out on stage:

Love is like a river
Ever flowing to the sea.
A never-ending promise
Living through eternity.

Everyone in the Tulsa Convention Center rose to their feet, clapping and cheering. The band played for a minute or two while Andi acknowledged their warm welcome. The audience quieted, but few sat down as Andi and Nicki continued the song. They finished to thunderous applause.

"Ladies and gentlemen, my friend Nicki Alexander." Andi stepped back to allow Nicki another moment in the limelight. When the young woman ran off stage, Andi caught a glimpse of Kyle giving her a big bear hug. "Thank you so much for that wonderful welcome. I'm so glad we were able to reschedule the concert, and I really appreciate you all coming out to see us. I think we have a good show, so sit back and enjoy."

The show went off without a hitch, and the audience loved the new songs Andi sang. They spent over an hour afterward talking with the fans and signing autographs. When the crew had completed dismantling the stage and had loaded all the equipment in the two semi-trucks, they piled into the buses and trucks and went to an all-night diner.

After eating, they hit the road, tired but happy with the success of the first concert. Andi traveled with two buses, one for her and the road manager, and the other for her band and part of the crew. The rest of the crew rode on the trucks.

Kyle had added another bus for Nicki's band. Normally, the singer in the opening act would have ridden with the band, but Andi insisted Nicki take the small, extra bedroom on her bus. Traveling on a band bus was sometimes fun, but it could also be a big pain. Andi had done it for years. The guys would have given Nicki as much privacy as they could, but it still would have been hard to sleep, and the band members were always playing tricks on each other.

Kyle had thanked Andi a dozen times for asking the young woman to share her bus. He was flying back to Nashville the next morning to finalize the details of Nicki's recording contract and had lingered on the bus as long as he could, parting from Nicki with a gentle kiss.

Nicki and Andi changed into their pajamas and bathrobes and scrubbed off their stage makeup. Too excited to rest, Nicki called her family to tell them all about the show.

Andi was happy things had gone well, but she was tired. And lonely. The ache in her heart never went away completely and much of the time it was almost too painful to endure. She retreated to her bedroom and crawled into bed, holding the cuddly teddy bear Wade had given her. "I don't believe he doesn't love me. He's just afraid I'll do the same thing his mother did. But dog-gone-it, doesn't he realize I'm not like her?"

Andi called Dawn from the bus as it sped down the highway. "Where are you?" asked Dawn.

"I don't know, exactly. Somewhere between Tucson and Boise. I don't know what I'd do if Tony didn't leave cards on the table every morning giving me a schedule and telling me what city we're in. The show in Boise isn't until Tuesday, so we'll actually stay in a hotel for a few nights. I'll be doing the usual phone interviews with the local radio stations. TNN "Country News" is planning to tape part of the show and do an interview beforehand. It's supposed to air on Friday."

"How are you feeling? Are you taking your vitamins?"

"Faithfully. I'm also being careful to eat right and trying to get plenty of sleep. I'm not doing so well in that department."

"Missing Wade?"

"Do cowboys ride horses?"

"Yes, and if it's any consolation, I think your cowboy has lost about ten pounds in the last two weeks. He doesn't look like he's been sleeping all that well, either. Ray said he's been kicked by a cow and had his foot stepped on twice since you left, and that he's been so grouchy one of the hired hands almost quit on Friday. I talked to Wade for a few minutes after church. He asked if I'd heard from you."

"What did you tell him?"

"That I'd talked to you on Friday. That the concerts were going well and Nicki was a sensation. I also told him you were miserable, but he didn't believe me. He said, 'Yeah, sure. She looked real miserable on "Music City Tonight." ' "

"Well, what did he expect me to do? Go on national television and let the whole world see that I'm dying of a broken heart?"

"Maybe that's not such a bad idea."

"Dawn, I'm not going to spill my guts over the air waves."

"You don't have to, but you could drop some subtle hints on the next "Country News" interview. Things that only Wade would understand. I know he tapes every show in case they say something about you."

"I'll think about it. Will you talk to him and try to find out the real reason he walked away? I know he loves me. I've thought about calling him and telling him how I feel. I'm to the point where I'd gladly give up my career to be with him if that's the problem, but I'm not sure he would believe it."

"Probably not, but I'll see what I can find out."

"Have you heard from Grant?"

"No. It might have been interesting, but I'm not holding my breath until he calls. I haven't had much time to think about him. Been too busy moving stock into my store and trying to put the stuff in the old museum into some kind of order so we can catalogue it."

"And you're loving every minute. I talked to my folks earlier. They should be back home in time for the Fort Worth show. That's going to be my last one, so plan on coming. I'll have them reserve you a front row seat, right next to Mom and Dad's."

"Save one for Wade, too. I'll see if I can get him to go."

"I'd like that. Gotta run. Call me if you find out anything."

Dawn called Andi Tuesday morning at the hotel in Boise. "I went out to see Wade last night. I tried to be subtle, but the man was as elusive as a roadrunner, so I finally just asked him out right if he wanted to marry you."

Andi groaned. "You didn't."

"I did, but don't send a hit squad after me yet. He's a good friend of mine, you know, and we talk about serious things sometimes. He meandered around a while, but this is what it comes down to—he loves you and wants to marry you more than anything in the world. Unfortunately, he has a couple of hang-ups. He couldn't stand for you to be on the road while he stayed home, but he knows he'd go crazy traveling like you do. He doesn't think he has the right to ask you to cancel or curtail your career, but I think I convinced him that you two could probably work out some kind of compromise."

"Of course we could." Andi's heart pounded with excitement and hope.

"Hold on; there's more. He believes that God will use your music and testimony to reach people that wouldn't listen to anybody else if they talked about Jesus. He's afraid that if you get married and settle down on the Smoking Pipe and raise cows and kids, that he will be thwarting God's greater plan."

"He's got it all figured out, without even talking to me to see how I feel? I never figured him for the martyr type."

"He's not. Personally, I still think it goes back to his mother, but he doesn't realize it or can't admit it. I think, even more than the fact that he wants to free you to do God's will, he's afraid you'll get tired of being married and leave. I pumped Della a little this morning about his mom. Evidently, she had a promising career as a trial lawyer when his folks first married, but when she got pregnant with Wade, his dad insisted she quit and stay home to raise him. She greatly resented being taken out of the courtroom spotlight. She agreed because at that time, getting a divorce would have been more damaging to her career than putting it on hold.

"She started back to work on a part-time basis against her husband's wishes when Wade was in the seventh grade. By the time he reached high school, she was in the district attorney's office and moving up rapidly. Her job took more and more of her time, until it became her whole life. She had always blamed Wade for what she had missed by staying at home, but, ironically, that anger and blame only intensified as she became more successful. The 'if it hadn't been for you, I'd be such and such by now,' type of thing."

"Somehow, I don't think he will believe me if I call him up and tell him I'm quitting the music business because I love him and that God says it's okay." Dejected, Andi stared out the hotel window watching cars come and go in the parking lot below.

"He might, but I doubt it. It's much better to show him with a bit of flare and switch gears with style."

"You obviously have something in mind."

"Obviously," said Dawn with a laugh. "Don't I usually come up with some of your best ideas?"

"And a few of my biggest bombs," Andi said dryly.

On Friday night, Wade stretched out in his recliner with a groan, then took a bite of the huge piece of chocolate cake Della had sent home with him. Two bulls had fought that morning, and though neither animal had been badly hurt, they had knocked down ten sections of fence. He had spent all afternoon digging post holes, setting posts, and stringing new barbed wire. Now he was bone tired and debating whether to watch "Country News" or just tape it. Dawn had called and left a message on his answering machine. He thought she said something about an interview with Andi, but the machine had gobbled up the tape.

He wasn't sure he was up to seeing anything about her. Sighing, he flipped on the television anyway, automatically turning on the video recorder at the same time. *Might as well watch it and get it over with.* Andi's story was the first on the program.

"Singer Andrea Carson continues to delight audiences as she finishes out the tour that had to be canceled a few months ago because of illness. Andi has taken an up-and-coming star under her wing, a young lady she discovered while she was recuperating in Texas. Powerhouse singer Nicki Alexander has been opening up the show and earning rave reviews and tremendous audience support. As wonderful as these two singers are individually, when they team up, they are nothing short of stupendous. And the fact that Andi shares her first moments on stage with the young singer speaks volumes about this woman's heart."

The scene changed to Nicki on stage with the band. As she sang the first few words, Wade recognized the song as the one Andi had written, although she had only told him about it. Hearing Andi's beautiful voice, he sat up straight and slowly set his cake on the table beside him, anticipating her entrance. Nicki sang again, then Andi, and when their voices blended in exquisite harmony, and Andi walked out on stage, Wade's throat constricted.

"Andi has always been energetic on stage, but these days her performances seem to be filled with a new vitality," continued the reporter. "Even when she slows the pace to do a love song or a ballad, she is vibrant. This seems especially true when she sings gospel, a new addition to her show."

When they showed a short clip of Andi singing an old hymn, she seemed to glow with an inner light, reaffirming his belief that God would use her and her music. It occurred to him that the only times he had seen her look more beautiful was right after he had kissed her—a pleasing but confusing thought.

"We talked with Andi and Nicki at their hotel this afternoon before the show. We'll share some of what they had to say right after this break." A list of their upcoming performances flashed on the screen: Tacoma, Portland, San Diego, El Paso, Houston, Austin, and Fort Worth.

When the show resumed, Andi and Nicki were sitting side-by-side on a sofa. The reporter asked them various questions about the show, working together, and how they met. They also talked about Nicki's new recording contract, with Nicki proudly saying that Andi had written a couple of songs for her that would be included in her first album.

"What about you, Andi? What comes after the tour?"

"I'm going to take some time off, then record my next album. I'm still working on songs for it. I have several ideas that I haven't had time to develop yet. And I'd like to move from my apartment into a house."

"Do you have something near Nashville in mind?"

Andi smiled softly. "No, it's not in Tennessee. I found the perfect place when I was home in Texas."

Wade leaned forward, studying the tenderness in her face, listening carefully.

"It's a beautiful brick rambler on quite a bit of acreage. It even has a white old-fashioned swing on the porch. The view of the valley and hills from the front of the house is breathtaking."

Wade turned up the volume to hear her over his thundering heart.

"It's the most beautiful place on earth. I'd be perfectly content to spend every day of my life right there."

"No more tours?" asked the astute reporter.

"My contract ends after the next album, so we'll have to see what happens. I'm not free to talk about any possibilities right now."

"Have you made an offer on the property?"

Andi's smile softened even more. "No. It's not for sale, but I'm going to try to work out a lifetime lease with the owner. He's a wonderful man, although he can be a little thick-headed, sometimes. I'm hoping he will listen to reason."

"I am not thick-headed," muttered Wade. Then he laughed, knowing that was exactly what he had been.

When Wade came in from work late Monday afternoon, a Federal Express overnight envelope was tucked inside the screen door. He opened it and found a single ticket to her concert in Fort Worth. An unsigned note was attached, apparently written by the clerk in the ticket office. "Front row, center stage. Per Andi, best seat in the house."

He glanced at his answering machine. The light was blinking to indicate he had a message. Excitement spiraled through him as he walked across the room. His old machine had died with Dawn's last message, and this was the first time he had used the new one. He had to stop and look for the "play" button, since he'd barely had time to skim over the directions. He pushed the button, anticipating Andi's sweet voice.

"You have three messages," uttered a monotone robot voice, making Wade jump. He glared at the infernal machine and waited. After that disappointment, he half expected the messages to be from the Highway Patrol telling him he had cows out on the road.

Andi's soft voice reached out and wrapped him in tenderness. "Hi, cowboy. This is Andi. Just wanted to let you know I'm sending you a ticket to the show in Fort Worth. It should arrive today. If you don't get it by Wednesday, please call Dawn and she'll track it down. I hope you'll come. It means a lot to me. If you clap and whistle loud enough, I'll take you out to eat after the show. Bye."

He grinned, then raised an eyebrow when the second message started to play. It was Andi again.

"I hope you saw "Country News" Friday night. If you didn't, watch it this second! By the way, God and I have everything figured out, so you can quit worrying. You're not the only one with a direct line to heaven, you know."

The third message began, and he shook his head, laughing when he heard her voice.

"By the way, in case you haven't figured it out—I love you, and I'm going crazy without you."

"I love you, too, sweetheart," he whispered, pushing the "save" button.

"I have saved all your messages," intoned the answering machine.

"Shut up you dumb machine, before I shoot you," growled Wade.

"You may play them again."

Wade stared at the whirring, clicking machine, thinking the robot voice sounded smug. Shaking his head, he turned the machine off and threw his hat on the kitchen counter. "Looks like we'd better get together before we *both* go crazy."

CHAPTER

Twenty

∝∾

Andi peeked out at the audience, her gaze zeroing in on the empty seat where Wade was supposed to be. "He's not coming," she wailed.

Kyle patted her shoulder, but concentrated on Nicki as she finished her fourth number. "He'll be here. He's probably just stuck in traffic. Oh, did you see that? Did you see the way the light sparkles off her diamond?"

"Will you knock it off! Quit gloating because the foolish girl said she'd marry you. If you don't start showing some sympathy for me, I'll tell her everything I know about you."

Kyle flinched. "You wouldn't," he said, looking at Andi.

"No, of course I wouldn't, but I could use some moral support right now. He's chickened out, I just know it." She turned her back on the stage.

"Now, hon, don't give up so quickly." Kyle looked out at the audience. "Isn't that him sitting down right now?"

Andi spun around and practically fell on stage in her effort to look. She sprang back and grabbed Kyle's arm, closing her eyes in relief. "He's here! He did come! He loves me!"

"Of course, he loves you, silly. Now, stop squeezing my arm so hard. You're cutting off the circulation." He grinned at her when she let go and opened her eyes. "Don't hyperventilate. Calm down. You've still got a show to do."

"Yes, slave driver."

"Excuse me, Miss Carson, but a Mr. Jamison asked me to deliver this to you immediately. He said it was very important."

Andi turned to the usher standing behind her and almost started crying. The man was holding a long green cushion, the one from the swing on Wade's front porch. A note pinned to it said, "Front row, center stage. Best seat in your house."

"Oh, Wade, you big romantic lug," she whispered.

"He also said to give you these," said a second usher. With a groan, he set down the largest basket of red roses she had ever seen.

Clutching the bulky green cushion, she caressed one of the rose petals with her finger. "Aren't they beautiful?" She opened the card and read, "Sorry I'm late. Cows got out. I love you. Wade."

"You're almost up, Andi," said Kyle. "I'll take care of the flowers and the cushion." He took the card from her hand and carefully tucked it back in with the flowers. "If you keep it, you might drop it on stage."

"When they bring out my stool, I want the cushion, too."

Kyle smiled. "That can be arranged."

She pulled one of the roses from the bouquet, then walked over to the cordless microphone and removed it from the stand. Nicki began their duet, and Andi came in right on cue, her heart overflowing with happiness. When she walked out on stage, the audience came to their feet. Her gaze swept past Nicki's family, past her own mother and father and Dawn, to Wade's wonderful, smiling face, clearly visible in the stage lights. He clapped and stomped one foot and let loose with a shrill whistle.

She laughed and walked toward him as the band continued to play, and Nicki waited patiently. He went still as she approached. There were steps a few feet from him going down to his level, but she didn't use them. Instead, she stopped at the edge of the stage, kissed the rose, and tossed it to him. Standing in the edge of her spotlight, he caught it with a smile and lifted it to his lips. The audience gave them their hearty approval.

Andi laughed in delight and scampered back to Nicki's side, so they could finish the song. After Nicki left the stage, Andi jumped right into the show, giving the performance of her life—for Wade, for her family, for the fans—because it might be the last big show she ever did. She felt a twinge of sadness mixed in with her joy, but she did not dwell on it. She was wise enough to know that at times she might miss these performances, but she knew God had something far more wonderful in store for her, both as a woman and in her career.

As Wade watched her sing and dance and entertain—better than she had ever done before—his soul rejoiced. He took pleasure in her accomplishments and joy in the knowledge that much of her happiness was because of him. It humbled him, too.

During the second half of the show, the pace slowed, and Andi shared briefly about her illness and her relationship with Jesus. "This is a song many of you probably know. Feel free to sing along." The keyboardist played the first few bars of "Amazing Grace," then faded out, leaving her to sing the old hymn without instrumental accompaniment.

Wade blinked back tears as her beautiful voice soared to the heavens. No one sang with her. It seemed as if no one dared breathe. He glanced around, looking at the people in the rows curving around the stage. Some had their hands in the air, an attitude of praise to God. Others sat with their heads bowed, tears running down their cheeks. Many sat with their eyes fixed on Andi as if they were listening to the words for the very first time.

Lord, he prayed silently, *if you want her to continue with this life, I won't stand in the way. I'll work with her to make it happen. I'll support her in any way I can.*

When the song ended, silence filled the coliseum.

"Amen!" shouted Wade in his deep voice. A hundred voices agreed, then the applause began.

Andi lifted her hand to the heavens, directing the praise to God.

A few minutes later, a stagehand brought out a tall stool and the green cushion. Wade almost laughed out loud. Dawn looked at it and leaned over to ask if it was the cushion from his swing. When he replied that it was, she giggled and turned to tell Andi's parents.

At Andi's direction, the stagehand draped the bulky cushion over the stool, then helped her climb up on top of it. She adjusted the microphone in the stand and strummed a few chords on her guitar. "I'd like y'all to pretend that you're with a few hundred of your closest friends, sittin' around a campfire somewhere out on the prairie." The lead guitarist howled like a coyote, and the audience laughed. Andi looked back at the band. "Don't start yippin', boys. Somebody throw him a bone." The drummer threw a gigantic sponge bone at him, evoking more laughter from the crowd.

She played and sang some old cowboy ballads and the one she had written about her great-grandfather. Then she sat still for a few minutes, and Wade's pulse rate picked up. Something important was coming.

"Since resuming the tour, I've been asked many times what has changed about me. No one can quite put their finger on it, but they know something about me is different, something is better. There are probably several reasons. I'm healthier than I've been in years. And I've gotten my relationship with the Lord straightened out.

"But there is something else I haven't been free to share about. I've discovered in the last few months that I've been lying to you. I've sung love songs for years and even written several that were considered pretty good. But I didn't know what I was talking about.

"Now, I do. While I was back home last month, I renewed a friendship with an old friend from high school. Friendship has grown into love. Even before I got sick, there was an emptiness in my life, a loneliness that nothing could ease. When I gave my life to Jesus again, part of that emptiness was filled, but not all of it. Because of the love of a very special man, now that emptiness is gone, and my heart overflows with love and happiness. That's what you see, that's what you hear when I sing. His love for me, and mine for him.

"I want to be a wife and mother, but I can't have the kind of family life I want and keep up such a high-paced career. I also believe God is calling me to do other things, although I haven't sorted them out yet. I'm contracted to do another album, but this is my last tour." She waited while the fans noisily digested the news.

"I want to thank you from the bottom of my heart for all

your support, both in coming to the show and in buying my music. I love you very much and appreciate you tremendously. I hope you'll continue to enjoy my music—and buy my albums," she added with a big grin. "And I hope you'll understand."

She looked at Wade and smiled, then glanced slowly around the auditorium. "Now, this cowboy of mine and I have had a communication problem, so I hope you'll bear with me while we get a few minor details straightened out. During a television interview last week, I dropped a big hint to him that I'd like to marry him. Of course, I couldn't come right out and say that over the air, so I indicated I was interested in taking out a lifetime lease on his house." Laughter rippled through the audience. "Then I sent him a ticket for tonight's show with a little note indicating it was the best seat in the house.

"I reckon he understood my hint the other day, because tonight he sent this cushion back stage. It's from his porch swing, the one that looks out over the most beautiful valley this side of heaven. There's a little note pinned on it here." She stretched down and lifted the edge of the cushion to read the note. "Front row, center stage. Best seat in your house."

The women in the audience sighed and the men grinned.

"He was late getting here, and I'd about given up. Then he arrived and sent this beautiful basket of flowers back stage." A stagehand hauled out the flowers. "It has a little note, too, apologizing for being late." She paused. "The cows got out."

Giggles and guffaws filled the air.

"Now, understand we haven't actually talked to each other in about a month, so I may be jumpin' the gun a little." She looked right at him, and his heart almost leaped out of his chest. "Wade, honey, if you're proposing, I'm saying yes."

He knew she expected him to go up on stage; it was the only way to end the evening. But his legs had suddenly turned to Jell-O.

Dawn jabbed him with her elbow. "Move!"

Wade pushed himself out of the seat and started toward the stairs leading to the stage, thinking he was grinning like a possum eatin' persimmons. He met Andi's loving gaze and his grin grew even wider. As he walked onto the stage, her face filled with alarm, and she scrambled down from the stool.

A man ran by, and Wade caught a strong whiff of alcohol.

"Andi, baby, ya can't quit! Ya can't desert us!"

Rage and adrenaline shot through Wade. He ran several steps and took a flying leap, tackling the man a few yards away from Andi. When the troublesome fan tried to get up, Wade slammed him down on the floor again and put his knee in the middle of his back, twisting one arm behind him. "Don't move, or so help me, I'll break it," he ground out.

Two security guards who had been standing in front of the stage reached them in seconds. Wade glared at them. "Why weren't you doing your job?"

The guards looked sheepish. "I-I guess we were watchin' you and Miss Carson," stammered one of them, reaching down to grab hold of the man, who was now blubbering about "no more pretty music to listen to."

Wade stood, partly using the knee he had in the man's back to push himself upward, feeling a small amount of satisfaction at the man's "Umph."

He covered the remaining distance to Andi in two long strides and gathered her in his arms. "Looks like I'm gonna have to marry you to keep you out of trouble," he muttered, not realizing he was right in front of the microphone until the audience laughed.

She hugged him, then looked up into his eyes. "You do such a nice job of it."

Wade grinned. "I guess I didn't do too bad."

Andi grinned, then tapped him on the chest with one finger. "I had decided you'd chickened out. Couldn't you let your cowboys put the cattle back? Just this once?"

"They weren't my cows." When she raised an eyebrow, he smiled and drawled, "Darlin', let me explain."

"We're waiting," she said, nodding at the crowd and the microphone.

"I was on my way with time to spare, but I ran into a big traffic jam. A cattle truck had turned over on the freeway. There were cows runnin' all over the place. I had a rope with me—"

"Always carry one just in case, huh?" She smiled sweetly.

"As a matter of fact, I do. Since I had a rope and knew what I was doing, I had to help. Those poor critters were scared to death and were liable to get run over."

"Well, we couldn't have that. You did the right thing."

"I do occasionally." He leaned down and kissed her, oblivious to the hoots and whistles of the crowd. When he finally ended the kiss, he smiled down into her eyes. Unsnapping the flap on his breast pocket, he said, "Andrea Carson, I've loved you since the first day I met you, when I walked into senior English class, and you smiled at me."

"I knew it!" shouted a woman in the front row.

Wade frowned, lifted his hand to shade his eyes, and peered

at the audience. Andi did the same. "Is that you, Miss Atkins?" he asked.

"It is, only it's Mrs. Garner, as of yesterday afternoon."

"Congratulations and best wishes," they said in unison.

"Thank you. I knew you were in love with her, Wade Jamison. You stared at her so much during class, you almost flunked English. It's high time you did something about it."

"Yes, ma'am. I'm tryin' to."

The audience went into hysterics.

Wade looked at his love and smiled. "I'm gonna get you for this," he whispered.

She grinned. "Promises, promises."

Slowly the spectators quieted down, waiting expectantly.

"As I was saying…I love you more than anything in the world. I want to spend the rest of my life with you, with or without your singing career. God brought us together, and I know he means for us to stay together." He dug a ring out of his pocket, a beautiful diamond solitaire. "Andi, my love, will you make my heart sing through all eternity? Will you marry me?"

"Oh, yes!" She smiled blissfully as he slipped the ring on her finger. When he bent down to kiss her, she slid her arms around his neck.

The crowd rose as one, clapping and crying and hugging each other, but Wade and Andi barely noticed. He was only vaguely aware of the curtain closing a few minutes later, but when he finally raised his head and spotted a television camera aimed at them, he began to chuckle.

"What's so funny?" asked Andi, gazing at him with sparkling eyes.

He nodded toward the camera. "Looks like I'm going to be a television star again."

"You don't mind?"

"No ma'am," he said softly. "I'm right where I want to be."

Dear Reader,

As many of you have probably learned, God often answers our prayers in unexpected ways. Over the past seven years, he has blessed me by allowing my six "sweet" historical romances to be published in the secular market. After the last one, however, I hit burnout. The computer gathered cobwebs while I came up with all kinds of excuses not to write.

For months, I asked the Lord for guidance and began wondering if my career was over. Then one day, out of the blue, an old friend called to tell me about Questar's new romance line. He put me in touch with my wonderful editor, and as we talked, I grew excited but cautious. I'd never written anything set in contemporary times. When it came to writing, I lived in the 1800's, not the 1900's, but when *Love Song* popped into my head, I knew it was the right story. Another gift from the Lord.

I live near Seattle, Washington, with my husband, Gene, and our son, Justin, who is almost sixteen. I grew up on a ranch in West Texas and have a deep, abiding love for the area and the people who live there. Writing about ranchers, farmers, small towns, and even country singers seems natural. Like Andi and Wade, I often long for the beauty and tranquillity of those wide open spaces and go home whenever I can—hopefully not in the middle of summer!

Like Andi, I found the Lord as a youngster but strayed from the path when I got older. When Gene and I sought him once again, God used the verse in Hebrews to assure us we had the right to his grace in our time of need. Our reunion with him was much the same as Andi's. What a wonderful, loving God he is!

I hope you enjoyed *Love Song* and thank you for your

support. If you care to write, I'd love to hear from you. I'll get back to you, although it may take a while depending on writing schedules and life. Thanks again, and may the Lord put a song of love in your heart every day.

To God be the Glory,

Sharon Hillenwater

Sharon Gillenwater
c/o Palisades
P.O. Box 1720
Sisters, OR   97759

Palisades...Pure Romance

Refuge, Lisa Tawn Bergren
Torchlight, Lisa Tawn Bergren
Treasure, Lisa Tawn Bergren
Secrets, Robin Jones Gunn
Sierra, Shari MacDonald
Westward, Amanda MacLean
Glory, Marilyn Kok
Love Song, Sharon Gillenwater
Cherish, Constance Colson
Betrayed, Lorena McCourtney (June)
Whispers, Robin Jones Gunn (June)
Angel Valley, Peggy Darty (July)
Stonehaven, Amanda MacLean (August)
Forget Me Not, Shari MacDonald (August)
Chosen, Lisa Tawn Bergren (September)
Antiques, Sharon Gillenwater (September)

Titles and dates are subject to change.

NOTE TO DEALER: Customer should provide 6 coupons and you should retain the coupon from the free book (#7). We will send you a replacement copy of the Palisades novel you give away via Spring Arbor, consolidated freight. (In Canada, contact Beacon Distributing.)

PLEASE FILL OUT:
(ON PAGE FROM FREE BOOK ONLY)

FREE BOOK TITLE _____

ISBN _____

STORE NAME _____

ADDRESS _____

_____

SPRING ARBOR CUSTOMER ID# _____
(VERY IMPORTANT!)

BEACON DISTRIBUTING ACCOUNT # (CANADIANS ONLY) _____

Staple the 6 coupons together with #7 and the information above on top.

You may redeem the coupons by sending them to:

Palisades Customer Service
Questar Publishers, Inc.
P.O. Box 1720
Sisters, OR 97759

Canadians send to:
Beacon Distributing
P.O. Box 98
Paris, Ontario
N3L 3E5

BUY SIX
GET ONE
FREE

PALISADES
FREQUENT
BUYER
COUPON

Applies to any Palisades novel priced at $8.99 and below.

Dealer must retain coupon from free Palisades novel.

Consumer must pay any applicable sales tax.

AT PARTICIPATING DEALERS